Stories

# Oregon Stories

Oregon 150
Commission

Ooligan Press
Portland, Oregon

*Oregon Stories*
Ooligan Press
Portland State University

ISBN 978-1-932010-33-6

Ooligan Press
Department of English
Portland State University
P.O. Box 751, Portland, Oregon 97207
503.725.9410; fax: 503.725.3561
ooligan@ooliganpress.pdx.edu
www.ooliganpress.pdx.edu

Library of Congress Cataloging-in-Publication Data

Oregon stories.
    p. cm.
"Oregon 150 Commission."
ISBN 978-1-932010-33-6
1. Oregon—Anecdotes. I. Oregon 150.
F876.6.O74 2010
979.5—dc22
                            2010003469

Cover Design by Elisabeth Wilson
Interior Design by Andrew Wicker & Chory Ferguson
Cover photos Copyright © 2009 Caroline Wilson & Elisabeth Wilson

For more information contact Ooligan Press at
Portland State University, Portland, Oregon.

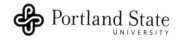

This book is part of our Oregon story. What's yours?

# Contents

Foreword: A Honey Hive of Voices  xiii
Preface  xvii
Introduction  xix

## Destination: Oregon  1

| | | |
|---|---|---|
| Oregon at First Glance | Jhana McCullum | 3 |
| My Oregon, 1998 | Elizabeth Danek | 4 |
| An Accidental Oregonian | Susan Castillo | 6 |
| Are You an Ore-fornian? | Cheryl Nelson | 8 |
| Left for DUNGENESS | Alexandra Marias | 10 |
| The Conversion | Jane Kirkpatrick | 11 |
| Changing Directions | Margaret Garrington | 13 |
| Oregon Rain | Carla Perry | 14 |
| Youngs River Falls | Anonymous | 15 |
| Absolute Ocean Awe | Mindy Mallams | 16 |
| Falling for Oregon | Tim Gillespie | 17 |
| Rain on the Siletz River | Kathleen Ritzman | 19 |
| Calling Oregon "Home" | Ellen Osborn | 20 |
| Oh Oregon | Christina Duane | 21 |
| The Best of Both Worlds | Robyn Burley | 23 |
| The Journey to Oregon | Ivan Ortiz-Bucio | 25 |
| Returning Home After a Crash | Molly Bandonis | 26 |
| Oregon | Hadeel Malak | 27 |
| The Stormy Beach | Myria Oldfield | 28 |
| Something to Celebrate | Heather Wickersham | 30 |
| Oregonian, Not Minnesotan | Glennis Peterson | 31 |
| From Barstow to Portland | Joseph Fitzgibbon | 32 |
| Destination: Home | Heather Wales | 34 |

## Outdoor Oregon  35

| | | |
|---|---|---|
| Oregon Story | Gov. Ted Kulongoski | 37 |
| The Alsea River | Sherry Cordle | 39 |
| Ona's Teeming Masses | Steve Snow | 40 |

| | | |
|---|---|---|
| Crater Lake Memories | Bob O'Sullivan | 41 |
| Oregon in Motion | Theo Lippert | 42 |
| The Wild that We Traverse | Katherine Rose | 44 |
| Detroit Lake | Jaimie Hays | 45 |
| Window View | Kim Hall | 47 |
| My Worst Camping Trip | Rosanna Dieterich | 50 |
| Oregon Rain | Eli Hermanson | 52 |
| Lost | Andrew Schell | 53 |
| My Home | Emily Garcia | 56 |
| Pendant | KatSue Grant | 57 |
| Fly-Fishing… | Monty Cartwright | 58 |
| The Little Heroine | William Minshall | 59 |
| Monet Landscape | Sara Fox | 61 |
| Dabbling | Cheryl Garrett | 62 |
| Alone | Sharon Sargent | 63 |
| Our Feet Dangle | Jessica Abney | 64 |
| Real Men | Andrew Harris | 65 |
| Rain-Fed | Barbara Houghton | 66 |
| Lost in the Tides | Taylor Richards | 67 |
| Olallie Lake | Nicholas Davis | 69 |
| An Experience at Skibowl | Eric Peterson | 70 |
| Rafting the Clackamas River | Andrew Schell | 71 |
| Multnomah Falls | Philip Nguyen | 73 |
| Just Squeeze | Melinda Jacobs | 74 |
| Cascade Head | Carol A. Hayes | 76 |
| Learning to Love the Sky | Mary Emerick | 77 |

## Young Oregon 79

| | | |
|---|---|---|
| Dearest Oregon, Happy Birthday | Tyler Nelson | 81 |
| Summer Days | Kayla Livesay | 82 |
| The Crater State | Ben Roebber | 83 |
| Playing in the Rain | Terra McClellan | 84 |
| The 2008 Snow | Gus McD | 85 |
| Fond Memories… | Harriet B.S. Guardino | 86 |
| Back Home | Mark E. Walton | 89 |
| Mabel's Journal | Alison Mae Lasher | 90 |

| | | |
|---|---|---|
| South Beach Jetty | Skylar Mathew Morris | 93 |
| Rain on a Friday Night | JD Bricker | 94 |
| Bigfoot | Forrest Murphy | 95 |
| Bethel Elementary School... | Kitri McGuire | 96 |
| Mighty | Anna Zekan | 98 |
| Life on the Willamette | Jackie Heifner | 99 |
| Summer of '96 | Tianna Munoz | 100 |
| Outdoor School | Lizzie Poetzsch | 101 |
| Crazy Stories | Jeff Lovelady | 103 |
| Champions | Landon Martinez | 104 |
| Beach Trip | Sam Harthun | 106 |
| Summer Picking—Summer Money | Jacqueline Potter | 108 |
| Epic Lightning Story | Mikayla Friend | 110 |
| My Oregon | Dallas Crone | 112 |

## Historic Oregon 115

| | | |
|---|---|---|
| My Oregon Story | Gov. Barbara Roberts | 117 |
| String Ties | Bill Hansell | 119 |
| That Remarkable Group... | Katherine Keniston | 121 |
| My Vision... | Jack McGowan | 123 |
| Pine Street Coffee House... | Julie Crossley | 125 |
| Questions for Grandma Carlson | Anonymous | 126 |
| The Sitka Spruce... | Ore. Travel Info. Council | 128 |
| Timberline Lodge... | Jon Tullis | 129 |
| Columbus Day, 1962 | Minnette Meador | 134 |
| Early Life on the Farm | Hugh Mount | 136 |
| The Reverend Robert Robe | Marcia Allen | 137 |
| Celilo | Rebecca Phinney | 139 |
| The Last Person... | Debbe von Blumenstein | 141 |
| Fort Clatsop | Sandra Ellston | 142 |
| Journey to Damascus | Sue Fagalde Lick | 144 |
| Volcano Weather: May 19, 1980 | Kathy Haynie | 146 |
| Oregon's Moon Tree | Ore. Travel Info. Council | 148 |
| At the 1855 Treaty Negotiations... | Antone Minthorn | 149 |
| School Kids and State Lands | Julie Lindstrom Curtis | 152 |
| Mill Town | Rob Hallyburton | 154 |

My Mother... — Carla Tomlin Mundt — 155
Planning My Oregon Birthday Party — Tracy Barry — 156
The Warner Story — Fred Warner Sr. — 158
Millsburg? No Way!... — Cornelia Seigneur — 159
A Passage by River — Constance Spiegel — 161
Seven Generations — Theresa Sousa — 163
Natives — M.J. Damewood — 164
Celebrating... — C. & L. Mundt, T. Paolucci — 165
Once Again... — Marie Melsheimer — 167
Women of the Oregon Trail... — Rhonda Gill — 169
The Passenger Train — Robert C.A. Moore — 170
My Oregon Territories — Dusty Hoesly — 171

## Modern Oregon — 173

Things We Take for Granted — Chris Hampton — 175
My Oregon — Dorothy Heath — 176
In Tune with... — Dawn Rasmussen — 177
Strangers... — Nancy Murphy — 179
Broken Bow Encounters — Bruce Tucker — 181
Three Muses... — Scot Siegel — 182
Fifth Generation Oregonian — Jennifer Larson — 184
Taking Oregon with Me — Jeannine Jordan — 185
Culture Shock — Melissa Smart — 186
My Mountains — Lisa Jacoby — 187
The Skate Scene — Geo Teodoro — 189
Oregon, You Are My Home — Suzanne Chimenti — 190
Getting Over the Blues — Janet Dodson — 192
Dundee, Oregon, 2009... — Susan Sokol Blosser — 194
Blazing a Trail to Oregon — Laural Porter — 196
Old Days — Judy Rice — 197
My Life on a Farm — Nolan Coulter — 198
From Ten to Sixty... — Ron Allen — 199
Superslime — Tim Leigh — 200
Seals — Sid Gustafson — 203
I Am Green — Warren Hartung — 205
Oregon Country Fair... — India Powell — 206

| | | |
|---|---|---|
| What Lies Beyond | Jon Dean | 207 |
| My Friend, My Love… | Emiko Koike | 208 |
| What Makes a Vacation… | Todd Davidson | 209 |
| Gilchrist | Kelli Luke | 211 |
| Rainy Day Joke | Susan Thompson | 213 |
| Fell in Love with Oregon | Jason Moore | 214 |
| The Oregon National Guard | Lt. Col. Alisha Hamel | 215 |
| Keeping It Fresh. Keeping It Oregon. | Doug Zanger | 216 |
| Of Mountains and Rivers | Rachel Kvamme | 217 |
| Oregon the Beautiful | Dena Hart | 219 |
| Finding Macksburg | Dorothy Blackcrow Mack | 220 |
| A Place to Play | Gail Balden | 222 |
| Oregon Born and Bred | Teresa Carroll | 224 |
| Murder in Paisley | Patrick Broderick | 225 |
| On the Farm… | Robert Mumby | 228 |
| It's Raining, It's Raining! | Lt. Col. Alisha Hamel | 230 |
| Grape Lane Poultry Farm… | Jayne Miller | 232 |
| Pickin' | Sandra Ellston | 234 |
| Grandpa's Jackknife | Gentry Cutsforth | 235 |
| A Glimpse of Elk City | Alexis Steenkolk | 237 |
| Sweet Memories… | Kevin Trees | 238 |
| Oregon in 2059… | Ethan Seltzer | 241 |

# Foreword: A Honey Hive of Voices

**W**ealth is story, not possession. To be truly rich is to have abundant experience with the kind of trouble that makes more of you. From a thousand forays to visit what you find beautiful and free—to mountains, rivers, nights by the fire, splendid hardship, long wait and lucky break, and other forms of kinship encounters with a place—you may distill a taste of honey more savory than any expensive cuisine.

In this book, an Oregon voice remembers the cold camp in the rain, and the scorpion plucked from the tent wall and taken home in a jar of vodka. It doesn't get much better than that. One voice remembers when the favorite childhood horse bolted and ran until she dropped and died. Indelible. In such a moment resides the seed for a compassionate life. Another voice offers us the moment on the hog line when a hook baited with herring and a whiff of WD-40 could catch a thirty-pound Chinook: "I was a girl and I could rig my line."

Alchemy works by utterly changing base materials into gold. That's the theory, but with lead and tin in the seeker's laboratory, the plan often failed to fulfill. And yet, in story, this principle often works. As one writer says here, "not everything is handed to you." You go forth into the world to seek among simple things, and the greatest treasure may have been hidden by neglect. Touch dawn with your full attention and darkness turns crimson and gold.

One way this kind of transformation happens is when benign memory loss pares away forgotten days and years to leave the nugget shining in your mind: in gold sunlight, you stand very still in the blackberry patch in Oregon high summer, while your brothers throw rocks at the beehive. They are stung to frenzy, but you are not touched, and the memory remains.

You will come to this story in this book, and to many like it. Such a moment surges to mind, and will last, will keep teaching, will be a form of negotiable currency all your life. "Let me give you," offers one teller after another, "this little story I will never forget." And once such a story is given, the listener, the reader will never forget it either. Thus the storyteller's theory of relativity: time bends backward to touch Now to Then. The contact sparks to make the circle whole.

Who would have thought an Oregon story could be a moment on a New York City street corner and a chance encounter with Paul Simon? In this book, among many such enigmas, you find his life-changing advice to an Oregon immigrant: "If you want a big city, try Seattle. If you want a town that thinks it's a city, try Portland." In this book, a governor cleans a gravestone, and a child does the lightning dance. We need them all, for no one voice can do the work of Oregon story alone.

Many accounts in this collection deliver quietly. I invite you to let them accumulate. You are not reading a book of high literature here. You are eavesdropping at the family gathering. You overhear a great line at one end of the table, a patch of story at the other—then "Please pass the bread...Is the salad gone?...Any more pie?"—and then another indelible line, another story you will remember before you fall asleep tonight. Sift these for your own savoring. If one story does not speak to you, turn to another. The one you passed over may return to your mind to teach you later. Nectar is thin, sweet rain. But workers are many, and honey is sweet.

The resume of a state resides in the sense of calling that begins when we are young: "Strawberries, raspberries, blackcaps, marionberries, cucumbers, Blue Lake green beans, and hops—I picked them all." Such a worker will not soon forget the roots of local bounty. The prophecies that end this book reside in such stories of childhood ventures, a time when hard labor was not easily distinguished from deep pleasure.

A state is many things, both known and almost known. Oregon is the official meadowlark and beaver, swallowtail butterfly and song of the martyrs, thunder egg and jory soil. But the unofficial dimensions underlie all we might proclaim or legislate. More important than policy is that quiet way we know what we are about. Love of places by individual children yet residing in the minds of grown voters brought us Senate Bill 100, which began to save those places. In this book, we taste the myriad tributaries of that love that gather to be known in laws and practices. A state continues to begin with little stories by individual voices. May this book remind you of your own stories, places, devotions at this "last perimeter of earth," this Oregon. Give bread to the stranger, and it shall return to you.

—Kim Stafford

*Kim Stafford is the founding director of the Northwest Writing Institute at Lewis & Clark College, and the author of a dozen books of poetry and prose, including* The Muses Among Us: Eloquent Listening and Other Pleasures of the Writer's Craft.

The Oregon Stories Project was conceived of as an inviting and innovative way for Oregonians to learn about their shared past, current lives, and hopes for the future throughout the sesquicentennial commemoration. Oregon 150 gathered and published a series of informative, personal, and exciting commentaries—from Oregonians, to Oregonians. Web distribution of submitted stories was augmented by television, print, and radio programming and broadcasts. All stories, including those used for broadcast, were archived at the Oregon State Archives as education source materials for future generations, especially for Oregon's Bicentennial in 2059. Oregon Stories came from every culture and corner of Oregon, from Oregonians of all ages. Through their participation in the Oregon Stories project, Oregonians were inspired to learn about and celebrate their state by getting to know each other. They also learned about what makes us all Oregonians at heart.

—Aili Schreiner
Senior Project Manager, Oregon 150

# Introduction

I frequently describe Oregon as a wonderful mosaic. If you step back, you see an expansive natural beauty from the Pacific to the Klamath to the Wallowas. You see one people, united in their commitment to protecting Oregon's unique quality of life, and proud to call themselves Oregonians. You see neighbors and communities—even in the face of difficult economic times—sharing an abiding faith in Oregon's future. You see the sum of our hopes and the history of our progress.

But what happens when you step closer to the mosaic? That's when the countless individual stories of work and family, love and faith, disappointment and triumph, change and tradition, and dreams and memories come into view. That's what you will find in *Oregon Stories*.

This is a collection selected from the Oregon Stories website project, which was one of the six signature projects of our 2009 sesquicentennial celebration, Oregon 150. Oregon Stories was a call to Oregonians to answer this question: "What does being an Oregonian mean to you?" The answers poured into the Oregon 150 website by the hundreds in the form of poems, essays, photos, videos, and audio recordings. Some were family histories. Some were deeply felt statements of belief, hope, redemption, or philosophy. Some were brief moments of joy or reflection waiting to be shared. These stories came from young and old, urban and rural, the coast and the high desert, first Oregonians, new Oregonians, and everyone in between. The Oregon 150 website became a virtual campfire around which Oregonians came to know and understand one another better. Every story was different. Every story had its own cast of characters, and its own lessons. But every story also had a common thread—that there is no better place than Oregon to live, explore, raise a family, give back, celebrate what was, and build what will be.

So I invite you to read these wonderful Oregon stories—to learn about your neighbors and communities, the pieces of our mosaic, and the portrait of a state and a people of which we are all a part, and that will forever be part of us.

—Governor Ted Kulongoski

# Destination: Oregon

In this chapter, writers from all over explore Oregon with fresh eyes, whether they are sharing first impressions, telling the story of their return home, or detailing a visit to new parts of Oregon.

# Oregon at First Glance

## Jhana McCullum

When I first traveled through Oregon, I was totally amazed at its beauty. Even along 1-5, its splendor overwhelmed me. I saw hawks floating on air waves high above rugged peaks, a clean blue sky, and trees that stood tall and proud, testifying of greatness. The air was cleaner than anywhere I could recall. I found no smog, overfilled roadways, honking horns, or endless crowds; just a great stillness that echoed in my heart. Patches of snow lay about, yet fruit trees were fully blossomed and dancing in a gentle breeze. The whole of Oregon touched my soul and stole my breath away. I cried.

Born and raised in Pennsylvania, I joined the Navy in 1965. I traveled throughout America—Atlantic to Pacific, mountains to valleys, farmlands to cities, national forests and parks. So many wondrous sites, each with its own splendor—but Oregon never stopped calling me, so I moved here in 1978.

Oregon is unique. Its history is still new, its cities fresh and clean, yet it remains wild and large as life. Oregon is peaceful, inspirational, and shares its beauty with all. Oregon still is what the rest of America once was!

# My Oregon, 1998

*Elizabeth Danek*

The decision was made. After an eleven-year absence, we would move back to the states—to Oregon. I found the beauty of the region and the pace of life a sanctuary. Within weeks, I secured a teaching position in Portland.

"Take only what's necessary," I told my family upon my return to Munich, and opened up six suitcases, telling my sons to "fill 'em" while I whirled in errands. My husband would ship a few more mementos and join us by Thanksgiving. Ten days later, amid tearful farewells, we said, "Auf Weidersehen"—until my older son heard the airport page: "Frau Danek, bitte, an Schalter Sieben." At "Desk Seven," officers motioned for me to follow them downstairs.

"Either you have a firearms permit or you can prove these guns are toys," they said. I dug deep into four x-rayed bags to reveal Disneyland muskets and model German Lugers. We were the last to board, and the dour passenger faces told me what they thought of the delay. The boys laughed all the way to London.

At Heathrow we took a bus to the next concourse, only to land in a queue for Abu Dhabi instead of Chicago. The clerk in Munich, probably miffed by all the crying, had written down the wrong gate. Another page: "Passengers...calling passengers..." and again we boarded our plane while agitated faces surrounded us.

At O'Hare we regrouped. We passed through customs with no mention of guns this time, though the boys' belt buckles set off alarms. We survived a spilled Coke and briefly lost my nine-year old at a comic book kiosk, then boarded—only to be hit by lightning at takeoff. Three hours and several complimentary drinks later, we departed.

Eventually, the pilot announced our proximity to Portland. With twilight approaching, Mount Hood was visible in a rim of lavender and white, and below us, the vast Columbia. Forest draped mountainsides; neat parcels of land fanned out; sailboats and lights glimmered across the river.

We trudged outside the airport, dragging six bags and three backpacks, and hit the temperate August evening. A small blonde cabbie grabbed our bags and easily heaved them into her van. She punctured the quiet by asking about our trip, and the boys started laughing. I cried.

"Heck," she said, "let's take the scenic route." With that, she turned the meter off. Rays of the setting sun splintered over the Willamette. It was several weeks later that I understood her circuitous gift. We drove through downtown, over the Burnside Bridge to view the city, over the Morrison Bridge to view the Hawthorne Bridge; we wound through neighborhoods, past parks, down Naito Parkway to see the last group of fountain bathers, and finally swung over the Ross Island Bridge before we headed to our apartment, where a low full moon hovered and the waters of a creek lapped at our exhaustion.

"You won't remember any of this," she said, but I do. With all my heart, I do.

# An Accidental Oregonian

*Susan Castillo*
STATE SUPERINTENDENT OF PUBLIC INSTRUCTION

I moved to Oregon from southern California when I was in my twenties. I didn't plan on making the move permanent; I just sort of wandered here the way many young people did in the 1970s. I am an accidental Oregonian.

It may surprise some people to know that the state superintendent of public instruction wasn't much of a student as a child, but it's true. I wasn't a bad kid, just indifferent about school—a daydreamer. I didn't go to college for several years after graduating from high school, and so I found myself working as a secretary at Oregon State University. My boss was a woman named Pearl Spears Gray, the university's affirmative action director. She was my mentor, the one who encouraged me to go to college and earn my degree. I went on to an exciting career as a television journalist in Eugene. That's when I put down roots in this rich, fertile ground. I became an Oregonian through and through.

Years later, when I was approached about running for public office, I can recall writing my very first speech. I wrote about my grandparents emigrating from Mexico to this land of opportunity. I wrote about my mother dropping out of school in the eighth grade—and that her dream for her children was a good education. I got so flooded with emotion, I could barely get through a first draft. I didn't understand why I was crying. Then it hit me. At that moment, I was fulfilling the American dream and now had a chance to give back to my state and my country.

Oregon has always been a land of opportunity—for the Native Americans who have cherished this land for millennia, for the pioneers who arrived in covered wagons in the 1800s, and for the many newcomers, like I was, who move here seeking a new and better life, whether they come from Mexico or Russia or California. Who, if they're lucky, will fall in love with this place, with its beauty and its quirkiness, the same way I did.

Oregon has inspired me in so many ways, has given me purpose and passion. This is where my life changed course in a way I never could have imagined. This is where I have been able to live out my dreams. This is home.

# Are You an Ore-fornian?

*Cheryl Nelson*

Ore-fornian \'ȯr-i-'fȯr-nyən\ *n*: Any native Californian who relocates to Oregon, falls in love with the place, and eventually decides he or she prefers the Oregon lifestyle better (for any number of reasons), so he or she ends up staying there forever.

I moved to Cave Junction, Oregon, in 1979 as a college student. I fell in love with the beauty of the surrounding mountains, the cold, clear creeks and rivers, the changing seasons, and the abundance of native wildlife. For the next twenty-six years, I was the definition of an Ore-fornian!

An even better element of this story of immigration is the fact that my future husband, a native of Seattle, Washington, was already living and working in Oregon—one could say we sort of met each other halfway (if one referred to a map of the U.S. West Coast).

We were married at the Grants Pass Court House in 1984 and began raising our two children in a modest home on six forested acres at the end of a long gravel driveway. Jim was employed by the local sawmill, and I found seasonal work at the U.S. Forest Service. While Jim milled the trees, I planted them. I sensed there was a nice balance at work. I would have been happy never to leave this oasis, but, alas, the economy was a driving force.

We lived through the tumultuous Spotted Owl conflict and regrouped for the new Oregon economy. This prompted a move to the more urban setting of Medford, Oregon. Jim diversified into a marketing/sales position while I pursued a bachelor's degree in English from then Southern Oregon State College in Ashland.

Our children attended Lone Pine Elementary and, after that, Hedrick Middle School. Their Oregon education culminated at North Medford High School. Son and daughter alike have gone on to achieve great things. Rika is pursuing her MBA in museum studies at a California university, while her brother Ty is hot on the creative trail—designing jewelry and clothing, and making music—he and his jazz band buddies from North Medford are a musical force to be reckoned with. Both of our children pay homage to their mentors from Oregon; both are proud of their Oregon heritage. Last year, our daughter chose the Halloween costume to beat all others—she went as the state of Oregon! Ironically, she was a big hit amongst an audience of mostly Californians.

Having lived in Sacramento for the past three years, I miss my "second home." I visit Oregon as often as possible (a five-hour drive when it isn't winter), and I've kept the 541 prefix on our cell phone in hopes of returning someday.

If the Oregon lifestyle had a motto, it would be: "Natural beauty throughout, naturally beautiful within."

Time for an Arnold-ism (in the plural)? "We'll be back!"

Note: Both of our children are native Oregonians now living and working in California. Guess they'd be called Cali-gonians?

# Left for Dungeness

## Alexandra Marias

As a tribute to *Muppet Treasure Island*, Tim had refused to refer to the ocean as anything but "the big blue wet thing" for days. This coupled with the fact that my back had welded itself into one solid ache while traveling from Montana to Oregon in two days flat did not make my mood a pleasant one. I was not homesick but definitely not enthused about our new home either. Newport: a small, wet, groggy town that seemed to be undecided whether it wanted to be aquatic or terrestrial. As far as I could tell, this new coastal village consisted of intersecting highways, car lots, rain, squashed, mismatched houses, and signs proclaiming, "Left for DUNGENESS!"

After a quick stop at our new garish, mustard-yellow house, we threw ourselves back into the car and made our escape toward the ocean. While we were springing out of the car and onto the slick path to the beach, a gust of torrential rain flew into my face and open mouth. Disgruntled, I trudged down the path after my family, staring at the mud beneath my feet.

However, when I lifted my eyes to the horizon, the gray, infinite expanse of water that awaited me wiped my mind clean of all anti-Newport thoughts and left me transfixed. Maybe I could deal with Newport after all.

# The Conversion

*Jane Kirkpatrick*

I t's said that converts become much more rabid than those born into the faith. That's true for me, having grown up in Wisconsin, but having "converted" to an Oregonian in 1974. Not long after I met my husband (who was born in Ashland), I took a leap of faith and moved with him to 160 acres of rattlesnake and rock on the lower John Day River in Sherman County. The remoteness and challenges there introduced me to the pioneering spirit of the past as told through Oregon's earliest pioneer women. Since then I've written sixteen books and traveled the U.S. and abroad telling stories, all but one based on the lives of actual people or events that helped define Oregon's history.

I've long believed that stories are the sparks that light our ancestors' lives, the embers we blow on to illuminate our own. Each time I heard about some fascinating pioneer woman, I wondered what her life had been like, how she endured, where she drew her strength from, and what she might have been able to teach me about my own contemporary hopes and dreams. These connections happened casually: someone mentioned an Indian woman named Marie Dorion who might have spent five weeks with Sacagawea and is now buried on French Prairie near Salem. Two Native American women married to French Canadians affiliated with fur-trapping expeditions, and both pregnant? They must have had something to talk about. But could they?

Answering that question took three novels and connections with descendants from Quebec to Astoria. I read a boy's essay, reprinted in a historical society journal, about his ancestor's dream to build a hotel along the Deschutes River, and how they accomplished it through their affiliation with the Wasco, Warm Springs, and Paiute people. I was employed by that very tribe, working in mental health, and I wondered how the native people told that story. Finding out taught me about integrity in seeking our dreams. The Antelope area's Muddy Ranch showed me that landscape is a thread tying all Oregonians together. Touring Shore Acres State Park in Coos County made me ask: what kind of woman would inspire this, and why didn't people talk about her? Reading a historical book about quilting took me to Pennsylvania, Missouri, and Washington State, and four books later, back to Aurora, Oregon.

These histories of endurance, of men and women who kept commitments and who honored community as they met challenges, have given me encouragement I would have missed if I hadn't moved to Oregon, if I hadn't listened to the stories and breathed across the embers an Oregonian's spirit of curiosity and wonder. Oregon's pioneers and the keepers of their stories have shaped who I am and who I might become. They've taught me this: ordinary lives explored through story offer spiritual insights and give meaning to our challenges. Such stories help transplants to this state become true believers in Oregon's greatness as they seek to find their own.

# Changing Directions

*Margaret Garrington*

In 1977 my first visit to Oregon changed the direction of my life. At the time I worked as a land use planner in Arizona, and Oregon was already on my radar because of the state's progressive land use laws. Oregon was often cited as unique in the country because of its strong protections for farms, woodlands, and beaches. In contrast to other states, Oregon had developed a structure for maintaining resource lands and sustaining the state's natural beauty for future generations.

An upheaval in my comfortable life seemed unlikely, but everything changed on that vacation when the Rogue Valley wrapped its green and golden arms around me and would not let go. I fell desperately in love with the rural character, stunning vistas, and warm welcome of southern Oregon.

In spite of myriad life complications, and leaving a good job with dire predictions that I'd fail to find one in Oregon, my resolve to return to the state solidified. Oregon was constantly in my dreams for five years before my cat, newfound husband, and I could make the long haul from the Southwest to the Northwest. Oregon embraced us then, shared its bounty, and still does. In the intervening years, Oregon continued to change the direction of my life by finding me a few new professions, and eventually a different way of living in an artistic community. All these years later, my pastel paintings celebrate the Northwest's rural spaces.

# Oregon Rain

*Carla Perry*

The water whispered at first
and found me among the low mounds
of Kansas strip mines, living in drought.

It padded alongside
as I scratched at the earth of Missouri,
perspiring on parched soil,
trying to be sensitive about hidden springs
as I peered into empty winter wells.

In Iowa the water enticed, cajoled,
then insisted
I dream about a land
where water fell from the sky,
the sweet song of rain, a calypso of deluge.

The melody of free water haunted my sleep.
Storm clouds came for me;
*Survival,* they said, *we know where you live. Follow us,*
and in my walking dreams
I followed them home,
back across the dry prairies of Kansas
and gold mines of Colorado,
up into Wyoming,
across the orange skies of Idaho,
following the hint of dank
to the home of mold, fog, rust,
this lovely water that falls for free,
this rain that needed me
to feel it.

# Youngs River Falls

*Anonymous*

I arrived in Astoria, Oregon, in July 1979, having just left New York City. I was a wide-eyed twenty-seven-year-old coming from a place where concrete reigned supreme and the sun never set, it simply disappeared. Youngs River Falls, a majestic waterfall, was at the back end of the property I lived on. I spent days sitting by God's creation, watching in awe as the water rushed over the rocks. It sure beat watching the New York City fire hydrants gushing water after having been hit by cars!

One night I sat by the waterfall with my girlfriend and my friend Steve and his girlfriend. All former New Yorkers, we were amazed at our good luck in having landed in Oregon at this place, at this time. In a flash, Steve jumped up, stripped off his clothes, and jumped into the water, heading toward the waterfall. After jumping in he called to me, "Come on, jump in too!"

I'm as competitive as the next guy, so off with the clothes, and in I went. I would not be shown up with my girl watching! As I swam to the waterfall, I saw my friend get to the waterfall first and reach up to grab at the rocks. He then quickly turned and begin to swim back to the place where our girlfriends sat laughing at these two kooks for boyfriends, swimming at night in cold mountain water. Steve swam past me, not saying a word, but with a look of absolute panic in his eyes. As I passed him, I thought to myself, *I will not only get to the waterfall, I will sit underneath it too. I'll show him!*

I reached the waterfall and grasped a rock to steady myself.

Or so I thought.

I had grabbed an eel! It slithered through my hand and back into the water. When I looked at the rocks behind the waterfall, I saw that they were covered with eels. I understood Steve's panic—now I was in a panic too!

I swam back with the sound of laughter cascading down on me.

# Absolute Ocean Awe

*Mindy Mallams*

I learned at a young age not to travel long distances in the car with my family. When you're the youngest child, crammed in the back seat with your two older brothers on the road for twenty-four straight hours, you can get stressed out. The constant back-and-forth bickering can drive a person crazy. Lucky for me, however, the Oregon Coast was our destination. This would be the first time I had ever seen a bigger body of water than Boyd Lake in Colorado, so the long drive was killing me.

I knew we had to be getting close to the coast. I could smell the salty aroma circulating through the car from the open windows and could feel the air moving through my fingers, silky smooth. The plant life was also changing. I was used to dry, flat, brown terrain. This beautiful scene was completely new to me. The thick moss covered the tall trees, and the wild ferns grew in every direction. Then there was a clearing in the shrubs, and through it I got my very first glimpse of the ocean. The water was crashing down over the rocks, and the white-capped waves were rolling onto the sand.

I stood mesmerized only for a minute, and when I recovered I begged my mom to pull off to the side of the road. I bounded out of the car and ran straight for the water with both of my brothers hot on my heels. The three of us played in the water, not paying any attention to the cold sting. We didn't care if we were freezing; we were in absolute awe over the beautiful Oregon Coast.

# Falling for Oregon

*Tim Gillespie*

I fell in love with Oregon when I was nineteen. The memory of my first heart-stopping glimpse was rekindled during our 2008 primary election.

Exactly forty years earlier, in May of 1968, I was a freshman in college in California, juggling studies and political activism. A consequential election loomed. Even though the voting age was twenty-one, I signed up to work for the campaign of an obscure Democratic senator, Eugene McCarthy, an antiwar candidate.

In May, a call came for volunteers to help in the Oregon primary. I'd never been to Oregon. With three friends, I signed up for a weekend of canvassing in some place called Grants Pass. I even razored off my few scraggly facial hairs in my "Stay Clean for Gene" enthusiasm.

My beat-up old Ford station wagon was our transportation. We stuck "McCarthy for President" signs on the sides, loaded up sleeping bags, and headed north on a Friday morning. After a long, tedious stretch up I-5 through the Sacramento Valley, we began climbing. California's scrub brush and oak trees began to give way to tall firs. When the Ford finally chugged across the state line into Oregon, the landscape was breathtaking. Dropping over Siskiyou Summit, I was stunned by the view: hundreds of miles of rolling timber, a thick carpet of evergreen stretching to the horizon, majestically beautiful.

After crossing the Rogue River into downtown Grants Pass, we found the storefront McCarthy headquarters bustling with young volunteers. We ate spaghetti on paper plates and slept on the floor. On Saturday morning, we were assigned precincts and handed campaign literature and lists of registered Democrats. We rang doorbells in tidy blue-collar neighborhoods, trying to convince folks to vote for Eugene McCarthy in the following Tuesday's primary. I chatted with retail clerks, retirees, and mill workers.

Most were civil—and many were itchy to talk—intrigued by McCarthy, a maverick taking on the establishment. I marveled at the friendly, engaged, and fiercely independent voters.

That evening, my friends and I were footsore and weary. We spent the night outside town at the home of local McCarthy supporters—a farm family who fed us a huge breakfast—then headed back south. Tuesday night we watched the Oregon primary election results on the dormitory TV. When it was announced near midnight that Eugene McCarthy had won in an upset, we whooped and hollered. Oregon became my symbol of enlightened politics.

That election didn't turn out the way I wanted, and the war lingered on. But that's another story. This story is about Oregon and my falling in love.

Six years later, after I'd graduated, gotten married, and become a teacher, my wife and I decided to move to Oregon. Lewis & Clark College had an attractive master's degree program, but I was also lured by my memory of that trip to Grants Pass. In my youthful conception, Oregon was a place of engaged front-porch chats, independent thinkers, and magnificent timbered landscape.

Ah, young love. We've been here since.

# Rain on the Siletz River

*Kathleen Ritzman*

Nighttime. Sleepless. Too many sounds outside my door to rest comfortably. I quietly shifted out of bed and padded down the hall to the new living room. When I opened the door, I could hear the chuckling hum of the Siletz River as it vibrated the soles of my feet. *Shouldn't someone turn the river off occasionally?* I mused. Having come to Oregon from two drought-stricken states in 1996, I could not imagine people wasting so much luscious running water.

Only a week later, I experienced my first Oregon January rainstorm. I know it rained for forty days and forty nights—and I had no ark! The front yard of my flag lot became first a gooey mess and then a lake. The Siletz River had a reservoir: my property! The river became a liquid escalator, creeping toward my home and carrying loot downstream: tree trunks, basketballs, children's toys, and even a forty-gallon glass aquarium. I worried about dead bodies.

Nervously, I waited for the sun to return and hid inside my home. One day, as I tried to drive my children to school, water seeped into my Nissan through the floorboards. I retreated to the second story of my house and called the school to explain that my children had been "flooded" home from school. "Don't worry," the school secretary said. "That kind of thing happens around here all the time."

All the time? I shuddered. Fortunately, we survived our first winter storm here. Eventually I became casual about our winter weather and then learned to love it for the rainforest it feeds. Rain and the Siletz River: partners in the beauty that is Oregon.

# Calling Oregon "Home"

*Ellen Osborn*

I'll admit it. It's taken me quite awhile to adjust to Oregon. At some point, I realized that I probably wasn't the first wife to be dragged unwillingly along the Oregon Trail. It's not that the rain of the Willamette Valley winter is hard on this desert dweller, but I learned that there is a fine line between curling up under an afghan in front of a nice fire on a drizzly day, and pulling that same afghan over your head and waiting for the spring—however many months away.

In the Southwest I was used to a pot of flowers on a patio for yard work; now I've learned to hog out brush, like blackberry and ivy, ending up with arms that look like I was on the losing end of a fight with a bobcat. I've learned that "sun breaks" usually last less than the time it takes to tie a pair of sneakers and get outside. I've learned that you can "garden" in all kinds of weather and that "shrub wrestling," or jobs like transplanting a lilac bush, are better done when the clay soil is like butter in the winter, rather than like a brick in the summer.

One winter, to keep my spirits ups, I wrote fake bumper stickers in my head: "Oregon—where the trees grow like weeds, and the weeds grow like trees." But just like moss, algae and mold, Oregon has kind of grown on me. The scenic beauty is dazzling, and Oregonians are passionate about preserving it.

The contrasts in our state are wonderful. Portland has a vibrancy all its own, and my small university town of Monmouth—where I can run all my errands within a few blocks of each other (banking, library, post office, market)—is the ultimate in efficiency. In Oregon, we have stark deserts and forests carpeted by ferns, towering mountains and the rocky coast—all within a few hours of each other. As Oregonians, we're still marked by the pioneer spirit, no matter when we joined the journey on The Oregon Trail.

I guess I'll have to admit it. I'm happy to be calling Oregon home.

# Oh Oregon

## Christina Duane

And so I returned to Oregon, just as I always knew I would. It was a promise spoken into my heart years ago as I stood at the bottom of the Siskiyou Mountains in tears, about to leave my newly adopted home. It seemed it took a lifetime for me to find my way home, and yet, it is as if I had never left. As if the Oregon wind that whispers through the pine, the granite trails that call my name, and the rivers that soothe my weary soul have remembered me as I have remembered them.

I was eighteen years old when I came to Oregon as a young wife and mother of one-year-old Jessica. It was a rough twelve-hour drive that turned into sixteen with a baby, a dog named Bear, and a bird. I remember the awe of coming down into Oregon, the red mineral-rich earth, majestic pines, and green, sloping valleys. But it was the people I could never forget. At Ashland Christian Fellowship I sang in the bluegrass praise band, and young mothers forged lifelong friendships singing and praying together, watching our kids wade in Lithia Creek, helping each other through the recession. My son Josh was born at home in a candlelit room in Oregon. He would later fight cancer and win, and will soon have his own little son.

That fateful night as I left Oregon, I vowed to return. Friends in California would ask me if I missed Oregon, and I wrote song after song.

*I Love Oregon*
You ask me if I miss the forest ferns and pine
baking pies from berries that I picked out on the vine.
I love Oregon, mountains that touch the sun,
rivers and valleys, forest and streams,
the place most people live only in their dreams.
Back roads from the Applegate Valley,
to the heartland rich and gold,

where the bonds will not be broken,
nor hearts be bought and sold.
If you want to see life take the back roads,
if you wish to be changed deep inside.
In this world so vast there are few things that will last,
you will find them on the back roads of your life.

Coming back over those Siskiyous into Oregon was no less difficult twenty years later with three of five kids still with us, my ninety-year-old grandmother, and every space in the car filled with everything that didn't fit into the truck. But it was perfect.

My grandma spent her last days with a smile and a glow on her face, watching her great-grandkids pick blackberries in the land she'd lived in when just a small girl. We were closer to Jessica and to my grandkids who had moved to Oregon, and friends who had been the subjects of my songs are still here. So I wrote a new song, "Oh Oregon":

Oh Oregon, your native people,
chant beneath the ancient falls,
I join with them, your pilgrim daughter,
I'm home, I'm home, the red earth calls.

# The Best of Both Worlds

*Robyn Burley*

Kansas City, Missouri, will always be home to me, and I love and miss my hometown dearly, but I feel mighty blessed to be an Oregonian. It's funny because not a lot of people express home as two whole different states like I do. It's exciting to know that I will always have family in both places.

Being born and raised for almost half of my life in Kansas City, I can honestly say that I've seen the many struggles of life. I began getting immune to the ambulances and fire trucks zooming past my mom's house during all hours of the day and night. I've been witness to lots of street fights and gang violence. Many robberies took place right across the street from our house, and sometimes they would occur even closer. However, it's not all bad, because even though being raised in a poverty-stricken area may seem like a never-ending battle to the next person, I look at it as a blessing. It has taught me to appreciate the small things in life, which for some people is a hard thing to do. It's kind of like looking at a cup as being half empty, or half full—only I get the best of both worlds, because even if my cup is half empty, my cup is still made out of crystals.

Moving to this beautiful state of Oregon has also blessed my life. I have my oldest brother and my wonderful mom to thank for this. Even though my older brother and I were honor roll students in elementary school, my mom still knew in her heart that she wanted us to have the opportunity of getting the best education possible. My eldest brother told her about Oregon, so within a couple of months we were all packed up and ready to go.

As soon as I took my first step onto Oregon grounds, my face lit up. I was only a seven-year-old girl and completely taken aback by how many healthy-looking green trees I saw. Everywhere I turned, it was like a painting of beautiful, bright, vibrant colors. As we drove to my brother's house in northeast Portland, I was in the backseat alone, with my feet barely touching the car's floor (I was a very petite child), and I had the biggest grin on my face and millions of jumbled thoughts racing around in my mind. I was a kid in a candy store, ready to explore the many things Oregon had to offer to a seven-year-old.

Every time I travel back home to Kansas City to visit, I feel so lucky to be able to tell my brothers and sisters about Oregon. I tell them about random weather we experience from time to time. I brag about the diversity of this wonderful state. I express my true feelings about how blessed I must be to have the best of both worlds. No matter where I go or where I end up in the future, I know for a fact that I will never forget this beautiful state of Oregon.

# The Journey to Oregon

*Ivan Ortiz-Bucio*

It was one long, hot day on the farm in Morelia, Mexico. My dad was planting crops when he realized his horse was too old and weak. They needed a horse to plant crops and make money. My dad and uncle were thinking of a way to buy a tractor, but there wasn't a job in the city that had good pay. My grandpa was also growing old, and he was too weak to plant crops by foot. They decided to drive to California. It was a long journey. When they got there, my dad worked as a farmer for four years. After they made the money, they went back to Mexico and bought the tractor. My dad met my mom and told her of the jobs and opportunities in the United States of America. My mom and dad got married and moved to Oregon, where my dad got a job packing strawberries, and my mom worked as a cook. Soon my sister and I were born. We're glad to call Oregon home.

# Returning Home After a Crash

*Molly Bandonis*

My clothes still smell like the sweat and food and grime and river water of Shanghai. The chilled air of Portland (that, on a hot summer's day, has only a third of China's unrelenting heat and humidity) is incredible, a homecoming. I'm riding back with Sam, both of us in an ethereal sleep state for the three hours between airplanes and home. Remarking on the trip, I'm heavy-lidded and noticing scenery whip by. A friend calls me, and I hazily recount the beauty of China and how awful the crash was—our tour bus jolting forward, a woman flung out of her seat and onto the floor with a scream—we clipped a car and broke a nose. It was a sharp reminder of how far away from home we were.

We're absorbing these recognizable roads, big trees, bordering-on-calm drivers, crisp air—Sam on over-the-counter, late-night trucker drugs, and I'm crashing hard from two days' lack of sleep. Oregon pulses as a waking dream I find I actually missed. Those three hours tender the best of Oregon I've ever seen.

# Hadeel Malak

The first time I came to Oregon with my husband was after we went to Hawaii for our honeymoon in 2005. Our first impression was: Wow; it's a very nice place, with all the rivers and trees.

Oregon is similar to my family's homeland with all the trees, hills, mountains, and clean atmosphere. Some don't like the weather in Oregon because it's raining and snowing in winter, and in the spring it is either not as warm as it should be, or it's cold and rains most of the time. But I am in love with Roseburg because it's the first city I came to in the United States, and the beautiful mountains look like lace ribbons.

For the people who don't like the weather, we have to thank God for all the generosity he gave to us, because many countries need water, and we are blessed with it in abundance.

# The Stormy Beach

## *Myria Oldfield*

Nearly six years ago, my mom, grandma, and I all planned a camping trip to the beach. We packed everything we needed and more. Everything was going perfectly. We woke up early and jumped in the truck with the camper behind us. I was so anxious I couldn't wait until we got to the beautiful beach. It was supposed to be a very warm weekend. On the drive over, we listened to music, and I even fell asleep when we were halfway there.

"Myria, come on, wake up—we are finally here," my mom said. I jumped up and looked out the window. It was the beach, but it wasn't how I pictured it. It wasn't warm or even dry; it was stormy.

We didn't know what we should do, so we ate lunch. While we ate, I only heard the crunching of chips and slurping of drinks. I looked at my mom, and then at my grandma; I could tell none of us wanted to go home. We all decided to continue with our plans for a great camping trip. When we got to the campsite we got everything situated for dinner, but instead of sitting in front of a campfire, we sat in the camper looking out at the wild waves. The waves were crashing hard onto the sandy beach. The rain poured down; it was almost the only sound you could hear, but to me it was peaceful.

After we had dinner, we cleaned up, and I found some cards. I sat down and began to shuffle the cards as my mom and grandma came to the table. At first we couldn't decide what we should play, but we decided to play canasta. The games went on and on—it must have been at least one in the morning when we finally stopped. We all picked up the table and went to bed. Even though I was so tired, I couldn't sleep. I looked out the window, wishing it would get warm so we could walk on the beach and run through the water; that's all I wanted. After I sat there for what seemed like hours, just watching, I fell asleep.

The next morning I woke up, and my grandma wasn't there. Neither was my mom. I looked around and called their names as I looked to see what time it was. My mom opened the door and asked me if I had looked outside yet. The sun was shining, and the waves weren't crashing. I was surprised that the weather had cleared so soon, but I had no complaints.

That was a great morning—I couldn't wait until we were done with breakfast so I could go on the beach with my mom and grandma. When we finished eating and cleaning our mess we walked—well, I pretty much ran—down to the beach. The sand in my toes, the water hitting my legs—even though our weekend didn't start perfectly, it ended up being the best camping on the Oregon coast.

# Something to Celebrate

## Heather Wickersham

Two and a half years ago we made the quantum leap to Oregon after living on Maui for twelve years. My husband and I dated, married, forged careers, bought our first home, and had our first child while living on the island of Maui. When we arrived in Oregon, we did not have jobs and had only brought our clothes and a few belongings. The past two and a half years have been consumed with finding new jobs and raising our daughter, who had her fourth birthday on April 9th.

It seemed like our time on Maui was a series of celebrations, and it seems like our time in Oregon has been a huge lesson in personal growth. However, the start of celebrations began to blossom this spring. It is difficult to ignore the fact that spring really awakens the soul. I can't help but have my spirits lifted at the sight of daffodils everywhere. A reason for celebration came this past weekend with our first hike with our daughter.

When my husband and I first met, we used to go hiking all the time, and we spent many weekends on backcountry hikes. After we had our daughter, the hiking came to a stop. We have spent the past four years talking about where we will go and what hikes we will do when Katie is old enough. The time is finally here. One of the biggest reasons we left Maui was to take advantage of the great Northwest, and we finally went on a short hike, with Katie leading the way, at Camassia Park in West Linn. We started the hike around the loop trail, and Katie decided she wanted to be the leader. The hike itself is only about a quarter-mile, but she went around the loop twice. She skipped and hopped the whole way, chattering about what a good hiker she is. I loved watching her hop along down the trail. The moment had finally come: here we were in the woods with Katie, and she was enjoying herself and having a great time. We finally had a "first" something in Oregon, and finally had something to celebrate!

# Oregonian, Not Minnesotan

## Glennis Peterson

In 1950, my birth mother toured the Pacific Northwest with a group of people, selling magazines door-to-door. She was from Minnesota. Three years later, as a single mom of a two-year-old, with no job and a baby (me) on the way, she wanted to leave Minnesota and remembered Oregon's magnificent beauty.

She hitchhiked to Portland, where she gave birth and relinquished me for adoption.

In early 1994, after a thirteen-year search, I found my birth mother still living in Minnesota. I needed a change of employment, thus moved there to work at a higher-paying job and to get to know my birth family.

Almost everything was wonderful, though I missed Oregon immediately. I loathed Minnesota's hot, dank, nasty, mosquito-ridden, tornado-filled summers. There was no escape, not even at night. Though Minnesotans have Lake Superior, it's hot and muggy there, too. At least Oregon temperatures are cool at night, and we are just two hours from the mountains or the ocean, where it really is cooler.

I missed Ducks football. I missed Oregon's beauty and comfortable climate. I missed everything Oregon.

If my birth mother had just stayed in Minnesota, I would never have known about living in Oregon. I hotfooted back after only six years, and will never leave again.

# From Barstow to Portland

*Joseph Fitzgibbon*

In 1968, after successfully petitioning my draft board that I was better suited for teaching than for trekking through the Vietnam jungles, my wife and I moved to the Mojave Desert and the impoverished community of Barstow, California, to begin a two-year alternative service assignment.

However, we were Ohioans and weren't prepared for sandstorms, tarantulas, or rattlesnakes, and certainly not for temperatures topping 115 degrees, nor the miles and miles of barren rocks and sand. Rosemary later remarked to her friends, "I cried the first day we drove into town and never stopped until we drove out."

By the start of my second year, we longed for all things green—trees, shrubs, plants of any size. Our conversations became obsessions for the splash of a cool stream, songbirds, butterflies, and even rain clouds.

"You'll find it up in Oregon," my building principal—a former Corvallis administrator—announced over lunch when I complained that desert life had left my spirit parched. As I stared out at the bleak landscape from my classroom, he filled me with images of Mount Hood, the Oregon coast, and the vibrant city of Portland, occasionally punctuating the conversation with, "Lots of liberals like you live there."

By Christmas break, we had our bags packed, road maps in hand, and infant son tucked in our vw Fastback. We headed north.

On our second day, we crested the hills overlooking Grants Pass and gasped. Heavy snow had transformed the mill town into a Currier and Ives holiday card. Although we nearly slid off the road, we stopped for breakfast, and listened curiously as several long-haul truck drivers urged us to turn back.

No way, we said. We were winter-seasoned Midwesterners, determined to see the river city, so we plunged back into the deepening snow. As marshmallow-sized flakes sent other vehicles to the roadside, we slipped in behind an eighteen-wheeler and followed it to Salem.

Three-foot drifts greeted us at the city limits, and radio forecasters predicted blizzard conditions by the end of the day. The schools were closed, but a stranded assistant superintendent offered me a preliminary interview for a teaching position, if we could find our way through the storm to his office. When we arrived, he greeted us with coffee and even offered to put us up for the night.

Cheered by such hospitality, we pressed on to Portland. We arrived just before nightfall and discovered a community pulling together to dig itself out. Young men helped seniors haul in groceries, good-hearted neighbors took meals to shut-ins, and shelters opened around the city to help out the homeless. It was the kind of spirit we wanted to be a part of.

We stayed for a week, long enough to watch the blanket of white melt, revealing hillsides of lush forests and rivers and parks so green our eyes hurt. We met spirited, energetic people who urged us to return. At the California border, we paused to snap photos of the "Welcome to Oregon" sign and knew without much discussion that this would be our new home.

# Destination: Home

*Heather Wales*

I moved to Oregon when I was sixteen to live with my older sister. I had come from the hot, pitiless streets of Los Angeles County, a place of flat, concrete buildings and endless roads, where nature had been beaten back mercilessly. In Hillsboro, I saw my first living animal that wasn't a canine or a feline. It was a sheep. It was tethered in someone's front yard, quietly trimming the vegetation as I gaped at it from my seat on the school bus.

The first time I saw a possum I thought it was a giant, mutated sewer rat! But I also saw places here that awakened a sense of magic in me. Here were green, shady nooks, cool and quiet but also wild. I wandered trails in woods that bespoke the presence of the little people my grammy used to whisper about. Daffodils grew on the hillsides, as well as bluebells of incredible freshness and beauty.

But here, I also found pain. Fourteen years ago, I lost my son, Logan. I carried him for eight months, snugly, safely, but one day without warning, his little life was gone. His death ripped me apart. I had to leave Oregon because everything reminded me of my baby. I left for years, trying to make a new home in Colorado, but my longing for Oregon at last brought me back. Running away from my sorrow did not heal me, but coming back to the place I loved helped.

I am one of those people who, though born elsewhere, embraces the name "Oregonian." My three boys also love this state, this town. We've finally reached our destination: home.

# Outdoor Oregon

*This chapter features descriptions of Oregon's vast natural beauty and wild stories of Oregonians' adventures in the great outdoors.*

# Governor Kulongoski's Oregon Story

## Ted Kulongoski
OREGON GOVERNOR

I came to Oregon because, like millions of others, I thought it was the most beautiful place I had ever seen. Rivers running wild and deep blue lakes. Majestic mountains. A rugged, wind-swept coast. High deserts, deep canyons, and broad-shouldered forests. So I didn't want to just live in Oregon, I wanted to find Oregon by hiking, rowing, and exploring its most wild and hidden places. My wife, Mary, felt the same way. We still do. But we've also learned this: if you want to see Oregon's untamed, natural beauty, get ready for a rough trek.

Our goal was to hike seventy miles along the Pacific Crest Trail. It didn't take long for nature to come knocking at our tent. Around midnight on the first night of our hike, we heard not just a thunderclap, but an Oregon thunderclap, loud enough to shake the ground. We knew what was coming next: a deluge.

How do you protect yourself from a downpour when you're sleeping in a tent, miles from civilization? Dig a moat. Put on rain pants, boots, and gaiters. And keep telling yourself: Oregon is as Oregon does. And Oregon does rain.

We woke up in the rain. We had breakfast in the rain. We packed our gear in the rain. We hiked south in the rain. And we got an eyeful of rain every time we looked up trying to find the sun.

The break came at Summit Lake, twenty miles from where we started. The rain stopped, but the clouds stayed and the winds picked up. And up. And up—all the way to the top of Cowhorn Mountain. Too tired, too wet, and too wind-blown to cook, we dined on M&Ms (the ones with peanuts) and prayed that the tent wouldn't blow away.

When we arrived at Tipsoo Peak, the highest point on the trail in Oregon, we had outrun the rain and were greeted by...snow. With the exception of one person—who ran the other way when he saw us—we weren't greeted by another living soul during the entire hike. It seemed like everyone else in Oregon knew better than to be out in the woods that week.

We descended the trail, still in a mad search for the sun. We found something else: slush and sleet. But we kept hiking. Kept our faces turned away from the biting wind. Kept inventing stories about imaginary forest creatures. And kept singing "Over the Rainbow." One day we hiked fifteen miles, hoping to find sun, fresh water, and a flat place to pitch our tent. We didn't.

After more than seventy miles, Oregon seemed to say: "Okay, you two—you passed the test." The sun came out and so did our smiles.

It's great to see this wondrous land at two miles an hour. It's great to face a challenge and get through it with your best friend by your side, and your sense of humor intact. And it's great to get home—and even better to call Oregon home.

# The Alsea River

*Sherry Cordle*

I met my late husband, Bob, while we were both living in Texas. Bob was a native Oregonian, and he was always telling me how beautiful Oregon was, and how great it was growing up in Albany and fishing for steelhead on the Alsea River. In 1993, we moved from Texas to Oregon to be closer to his aging parents.

Bob took me fishing for steelhead on the Alsea the first Christmas we were here. He had told me numerous stories about what fighters these fish were, and how tricky it was to catch them. About ten minutes after we cast our lines in the water, I got a fish. It took me about thirty seconds to bring that fish in. It wasn't thrilling like he had said it would be, and I told him so.

The next day, I got another fish on, only this time it was a twelve-pound native hen. She was a fighter. She did a tail-walk across the river and it took me thirty minutes to bring her in. According to the locals who were fishing beside us, she was the largest native to be caught on that part of the river in years. Bob was right—it was the ultimate thrill.

Bob passed away from Lou Gehrig's disease in December 2006. I spread his ashes in the Alsea where I caught that great fish. I like to think that he is there to help others experience the thrill of catching steelhead like I did. Thank you, Bob, for bringing me to this beautiful state. I miss you!

# Ona's Teeming Masses

*Steve Snow*

I run my Border Collies on an open beach with no fences. No one is here. We see birds gathered around something washed up on the sand. A bald eagle stands on top of a spawned-out Chinook salmon. The eagle watches my curious dogs. I call them, and the eagle resumes pulling red meat from the carcass. The eagle is very big; the salmon is very big. Further down the beach, logs are piled up. The logs have no marks except rounded ends from years in the surf. No footprints here either but my own and those of my dogs.

The rain stops and the sun breaks through the fast-passing clouds; still, I see no one. There are houses on the cliff. There are stairs leading down from them to the sand. Perhaps the people in the houses are painting watercolors and looking out of their windows. Perhaps they are sipping hot green tea. Perhaps they are shaping molten glass into vases. Maybe they come here at different times, secretly, so they can hear themselves better or see the world more clearly. Perhaps they are typing words.

## Bob O'Sullivan

My fondest memory of Crater Lake is of skiing there during the late 1930s. In those days Washington's and Lincoln's birthdays were separate holidays rather than the single Presidents' Day now in vogue. This arrangement sometimes provided a three-day holiday, during which a group of eight to twelve of us young folks from Klamath Falls could enjoy an extended ski trip to Crater Lake.

In those days there were none of the present-day amenities—no lifts or groomed trails. Taking turns, we would shuttle our cars from park headquarters to the crater rim. There were two trails that led back to park headquarters: a so-called "Novice Trail" winding down gentle slopes, and the more difficult "Canyon Trail" that cut through trees and down steep slopes. There was also a little-used cross-country trail, which extended seven or eight miles from the crater rim to the park entrance at Annie Springs.

Our equipment, too, was primitive by today's standards. Those were the days of leather boots, leather bindings, and long skis. The length of the narrow, wooden skis was determined by standing in position with arms extended up to the ski tips. The determined length, combined with the inflexible leather bindings, offered little precise control on the slopes.

One of the buildings at Park Headquarters was a three-story dormitory used to house workers during the summer season. This dormitory had one floor for women and one floor for men and was available to the public during the ski season. Cots, without bedding, rented for sixty-five cents a night. (The park rangers closely monitored the dormitory!)

Breakfast and dinner were available for eighty-five cents and, on weekends, the operator provided coffee and sandwiches during the day. Wonderful times, and the price was right!

# Oregon in Motion

*Theo Lippert*

I am standing still, watching.
Before my wondering eyes
the Oregon earth is moving.

Crater Lake seems to sleep
in its saw-toothed ring,
a jeweled, majestic caldron
that mirrors the subtle yet
cataclysmic changes
still defining the Cascades.

Glaciers have torn apart
Mount Washington, leaving
a jagged spire to pierce
the sky as if daring more
eroding snow and rain.

I am standing still, listening.
The sound of gravity-drawn rocks
tumbling, infinitesimal segments,
signal the constant dismantling
of one volcanic mount while
the Sisters push ever higher.

The rivers carry the rocky waste
mile after mile, grinding
boulders into pebbles and those
stones into grains of sand.

The rivers are born of creeks,
themselves the accumulation of
a myriad of rivulets, each worthy
of carrying a name as colorful
as its moving, purling gravel.

The rush of water merely
veils the groaning and gnashing
of the host mountains, as Oregon
constantly redistributes itself.

# The Wild that We Traverse

*Katherine Rose*

Ancient REI, Columbia, GORE-TEX, and other well-worn articles of outdoor gear collect themselves at the doorway from the recesses of our basement. The bright aqua and cool greens of the thrift-store-special equipment wear the scars of the wild places they have traversed. The small threads of the backpacks and tents have pulled themselves loose from their seams, while patches—with a slightly desperate appearance—attempt to savor the dying moments of well-worn travelers. Here up the valley, our home lies only a few miles from a tiny town of about 650 people. If there is one thing that I love about this place, it's a town where everyone knows everyone else, and one cannot hope to walk down the street without seeing at least three familiar people. There is a beauty in that.

We pack baked potatoes, water, random cereal, and dried fruit and nuts, and gather the dogs for the expedition. The temperate rainforest that spreads around us for miles seems to be waiting: a playground of cedar, scraggly Douglas fir, maple, oak, alder, and hemlock, with a sea of undergrowth filled with lush sword ferns and salal. My older brother, a couple of friends, and I, the only girl, know these hills well, but today we set a new course across our own corner of the Coast Range, down into the small river valley, satisfyingly soaking ourselves in the mass of greens. Sodden bits of nurse logs provide soft landing spots for the dogs and for us. We hack through the foreign, wet, earthy wonders, our feet slipping and our shouts filling the place with childish cries. Giant mountain salamanders, red-legged frogs, cave crickets, and small field mice scuttle beneath us as a majestically proud red-tailed hawk soars above. This is our home, this is our Oregon, and this is me.

*Jaimie Hays*

The sun was on my face and the water was slowly putting me to sleep. The dock was rocking back and forth, and I could hear the ducks swimming a couple of feet away. I was almost asleep when a splash of cold water hit my face. I jumped up. I heard a little giggle from my left, and when I looked, I saw a little girl's head coming out of the water. She was all smiles.

Detroit Lake is my favorite place in the world. It's a place where I can just let things go. I don't have to worry about anything except for getting sunburned. My family has a private campsite, and we try to go as often as possible. The weekends that my family and I go camping are the ones that I live for. When my parents ask what I want to do over the weekend, the first thing that comes to my mind is camping.

My favorite thing about the lake is being able to go out on the dock and let all my problems go away. I know that, when I get back home, my problems will still be there waiting for me, but when I'm on the dock my problems seem to disappear, and I don't need to worry about them. My second favorite thing about being up at the lake is hanging out with my friends and family. During the school year, I only talk to my friends, and my family is just an obstacle that stops me from talking to my friends. But in the summer, when I'm camping with my family, it's our time to talk and catch up.

At night, after the sun has set and stars seem to light up the night, I go down to the dock and look at the one thing most people can't see: the Milky Way. No, not the candy bar—the galaxy. Lying on my back on the dock, I can see millions and millions of stars, and above the trees I can see the Milky Way. There is no way to describe how beautiful it is.

When Sunday morning arrives and I can hear my dad walking on our deck and starting to put things away, I always wish I had a time machine so that I could make it Friday again. I stay in my sleeping bag until the very last moment. It makes me so sad to think about having to get up and start packing, and sitting in a car for two hours doing nothing; I have to say goodbye to the lake until the next available weekend. On those days, I wish it was Friday, and the lake was slowly putting me to sleep again.

# Window View

## Kim Hall

Iboarded the 8:30 morning train in Klamath Falls, headed for Salem. Stepping onto the train with my black bag, I looked for a seat next to a window. Several passengers had boarded the train with me, so I quickly took a nearby seat. This proved to be a wise choice, as it was a window seat that gave me a fantastic view from the left side of the train. With all the rain and snow the Cascades had been receiving, I was certain I was going to be in for a treat.

Once the train pulled out of Klamath Falls and began its journey, Klamath Lake was the first of many treasures along the way. I was mesmerized by the beauty from my window. The lake was calm and frigid looking. The birds seemed to be mesmerized as well, as they drifted restlessly in the still blue-gray waters. Once past the lake, farms and ranches were spread out in the fields of snow. Some of the homes were very extravagant, but most were weathered and rundown. One of the farm fields had a graveyard of broken-down vehicles and farm equipment. I wondered if the equipment would forever litter that small piece of land.

The train made its first stop in Chemult, where two passengers were waiting to board the train. A van with "Redmond Amtrak Shuttle" painted on the side was parked in the plowed parking lot. A man with a nicely trimmed beard, dressed in brown coveralls and a gray stocking cap, passed by my seat with his bags in hand. As I looked out the window, he left the train and the driver of the van took his bags. They drove off down the narrow lane of packed snow.

As the train rolled and swayed down the tracks, I could see Highway 97 in the distance, but as we began to enter the mountains, the highway could no longer be seen and a river replaced it, winding in and out of view. At times the river would completely disappear under a fluffy white blanket of snow, then reappear in full force, raging with dirty brown water over the hidden rocks under its path.

Higher up in the mountains, a post stood straight and narrow in a snow bank. The snow was up to the number six on the post. As the mountain became steeper on the side of the tracks, waterfalls of varying shapes and sizes appeared outside my window. No one on the train seemed to be looking out the windows but me. It was all I could do not to shout, "Look what you people are missing!" There were too many waterfalls to describe, but my favorite was nearly thirty feet wide and as tall as the mountain itself. The water came cascading down in white ripples, yet I could see through the water to the mossy green rocks that were part of the mountain.

As the train moved along, the deep snow lay across the forest floor, hiding beneath it rocks, logs, and brush. The limbs of the trees hung heavy with snow that sparkled from their branches. Now and then, small animal tracks would meander through the forest and disappear with no sign of the life that left the trail. The rolling carpet of white would suddenly disappear, and in its place a deep pool of dark blue water would reflect the train rolling by.

For many miles, the train rolled in and out of tunnels. As we neared Oakridge, the scenery became breathtaking. Suddenly, we were on a bridge going over Highway 58 as the creek ran beside the highway. The creek was wide and roaring, and it disappeared as we entered a deeper part of the forest. Smaller creeks sprang up from everywhere. Waterfalls, walking paths, and footbridges appeared. Further down the track, houses and shops lined both sides of the track. I saw a building with "Oakridge Museum" painted on the side. Further north of Oakridge, I saw a sign that read "Buckhead Wildlife Area." The train began to slow, and we stopped outside the town. An Amtrak employee could be seen walking along the side of the train, looking under it—for what, I did not know. Dusk was approaching, and I was anxious for the train to start the journey again so I wouldn't lose any of the sights to darkness.

When the train began moving again, the creek roared beside the train until we approached the reservoir near Dexter. Highway 58 could be seen outside my window, and the best view now seemed to be on the right side of the track, as the large body of water stretched as far as I could see.

Sometime around 5:30, darkness set in and the interior lights of the train came on, making it impossible to see any more of the view. Two hours later I stepped off the train in Salem, wishing I could take the exact same journey again the following day—but this time, seated on the right side of the train, to see what wonders lay outside its window.

# My Worst Camping Trip

### Rosanna Dieterich

When summer is fast approaching, my longtime friend Debbie and I begin to think about planning summer camping trips. Debbie and her family have recently moved back to Douglas County after living in Alaska, Washington, and Portland. We were both born and raised in the Roseburg area, so we know plenty of places about an hour's drive from home to camp.

The subject of camping almost always brings up our memories of our "camping trip from hell," as we like to call it. It started out just fine. We loaded everything up on a Friday afternoon, including Debbie's horse, and headed to Glide and up Little River. After unloading the horse and tethering him to a nearby tree, we went about setting up camp. When we were done setting up the tent and getting things put away, we took a break at the picnic table.

All of a sudden the horse went wild. He was in the middle of our camp bucking and kicking as if he were in a rodeo. The rope had gotten tangled between his legs, and he was in a panic trying to free himself from the rope, but only succeeded in getting more tangled. Mark, Debbie's husband, tried to jump on the horse, but ended up just hanging from its neck. They both ended up in a tangled pile on the ground. Nobody was hurt, thankfully, but that was only the start of things.

That night it began to pour down rain. My husband and I took refuge for the night in our vw Baja. The next morning, as we warmed ourselves around the fire, Debbie's five-year-old nephew took a tumble backwards into it. Luckily, he only received a small burn on his bottom. I think it scared him (and us) more than anything.

In the afternoon it warmed up enough so we could go for a swim. Somehow, as I dove under the water, I got hung up on the rock ledge at the bank and couldn't get to the surface. I finally managed to get my head above water, but that ended my swimming for the day.

Later that night, as we sat in the tent playing cards, we noticed what we thought was a shadow on the wall of the tent next to where Debbie's nephew was sleeping. Upon further investigation, we discovered it was a scorpion. It is now a pickled scorpion, having been placed in a jar and covered with hundred-proof vodka.

By Sunday morning I think we were all happy to break camp and head for home. Now, more than twenty years later, we think about that trip and laugh. I'm hoping our camping trips this summer don't involve crazy horses, children falling in fires, near-drowning, and scorpions—but, being in Oregon, they might include some rain. But that's okay. I look forward to spending time with my friends and family here in Oregon.

# Oregon Rain

*Eli Hermanson*

Outside the air is fresh and crisp, like breathing in cold air from a freezer. It is early morning, and there is a thick layer of snow on the ground and some in the trees. The snow has been covered with a half-inch layer of freezing rain from the night before. These conditions are very deadly to power lines and cars, and playing in the snow is only fun for a while.

Rain is one of the best ways to get rid of all the snow and ice. If you live in Oregon, you get plenty of the liquid falling from the sky, and all you need is a solid day of rain to dissolve almost any amount of snow. Anyone who likes the rain should live in Oregon, because we get so much that everyone gets sick of it at some point. But no one can stay mad at the rain; it helps so many people and only hurts a few—and they're usually up in Washington.

# Andrew Schell

I t was July 3rd, 2003, a normal summer day out in the country at my dad's house in Estacada. I was eleven, and my two sisters, Chelsea, also eleven, and Jessie, who was seventeen, were hanging out at our house with their friend Kayla, who was also seventeen. We decided we all wanted to go swimming in the creek, which was down about a mile behind our house. It was too far for us to walk, so we decided to try to fit four people on one four-wheeler. It wasn't comfortable, but we were able to fit.

The creek that we were going to had a pretty slow current and a deep swimming hole, so it was perfect to swim in. The creek divided the forest behind my house. This forest was full of green leaves, sharp needles, and ankle-scratching bushes every which way you looked.

To get to the creek, we had to take a trail leading through the forest. The trail led to many different places, so it was sometimes very hard to remember which trail was the right one back to our house. We all swam for a while, just having fun like any other kids would. As the day ended, we started to head back up to our house, but there was a steep hill that I didn't want to ride up on the four-wheeler. So I decided to run ahead, figuring that the others would catch up pretty fast.

Time went by as I was jogging up the trail, and I realized that I hadn't seen or heard the others behind me yet. I stopped jogging and tried to listen for them, but I heard nothing. I figured that they were fine and I would probably see them soon, so I kept jogging, looking for the trail that led to my house. It was the first time that I had ever been down that trail, so I was very unfamiliar with the land. I kept going until I realized that there wasn't any way we lived that far away from the creek.

I turned around, thinking I would just run into my sisters and Kayla as they were coming up the trail, but I went all the way down to the creek and never saw them. At that point, I began to panic. I started to make my way back up the trail, looking once again for the trail that led back to my house, but I didn't recognize any of them. I ran back and forth, up and down, looking for my sisters and her friend, or for a clue of something that led to my house, but I found nothing that would help me.

I began to realize that I was lost. There I was, an eleven-year-old boy by himself in the middle of the forest with only wet shorts, sandals, and a wet towel on his back. The day was quickly coming to an end, with the orange sunset complementing the blue summer skies. As I was searching for the trail to my house, and having no luck finding it, I decided that the best thing I could do was to get myself out of the forest and find a house or someone who would be able to help me.

As I was walking down the trail, I found a pathway where it seemed to me like there had been a lot of activity by animals, or even better, people. I decide to follow the path, and found a tall fence that surrounded a field full of cows. The fence was surrounded with barbed wire, but I knew I didn't have much choice but to climb it. Cutting my ankle, scraping my shins, I made it over the fence. I went through the field and over another fence to find a little old house with a barn sitting next to it. I didn't see any cars parked outside, but I figured I would try to see if anyone was home to help me.

I walked slowly toward the house, looking for a hint that someone was home. As I was walking past the barn to the house, I saw three rottweilers—the biggest rottweilers I had ever seen. I stood there for a few minutes, contemplating my next move. Then I walked toward the house at a very slow pace and knocked on the door, only to get no answer. I had no choice but to test my fate, creep by the dogs once more, and walk out the driveway to a long, empty country road.

As I walked for a while down the road, I recognized a golf course that my sister had worked at the summer before. I knew where I was now. I was four miles from my house, but I had no cell phone or any way of communicating with anyone at home, so I just kept walking in the direction of my house. I was no longer lost, but still, no one knew where I was. I hated the thought of my sisters and parents looking for me for hours.

I had made it about a mile and a half past the golf course when a white Ford Explorer slowed down and then stopped just in front of me. It was a

Clackamas County deputy sheriff, one of the cops who had been called to search for me. He asked me my name, my father's name, and where I lived. He told me that a lot of people were looking for me and that he would take me home.

As I arrived home, I was met by my sisters, who were crying. My parents were on their way home from work. Everyone had been panicking because I had been missing. They were relieved when I showed up in a police car. I was glad to be home with my family again. I still remember that whole day now, and the cop who saved me. Now I wish to be a police officer someday, bringing home a lost child, and bringing happiness to a family the way that heroic officer brought it to mine.

# My Home

*Emily Garcia*

When my family moved to Oregon, I was about six years old. My family moved sometime in the summer, when the sun was nice and warm and reminded me of California, but the air was much fresher. Before Oregon, I lived in Seattle for a year or two and often visited our family in California. My mom's parents moved to Oregon City, and we visited them a couple of times. My family loved the weather, so we moved to Oregon City, too.

What I love the most about living in Oregon is that you can have all the seasons in one day. My favorite season is spring. It's the allergy season, but the bright colors, clear blue sky, and singing birds make up for it. The spring is like a fresh start, a new beginning. My second favorite is fall. The sun is still shining on the changing leaves of the trees. The beauty of fall is colored leaves gracefully dancing with the wind down to the ground. Winter feels like a dream; frost sparkles on everything that gets in Jack Frost's way. And you can't forget Oregon showers that clean the streets and leave a beautiful rainbow that spreads across the blue sky. No matter where I go, or how long I have been there, Oregon will always be my lovely home.

*KatSue Grant*

I can see the Umpqua River
from my kitchen breakfast nook
easier in the autumn, winter, spring
when full and gray or brown,
greenish, gritty with silt.

I can see it from the grass of the glen
but by the western boundary's cedar tree
is best, with Mount Rose's knob behind it,
bright green pastures to east and north,
four ranges layered into the west.

Winter, it's funnel-shaped,
bottle-necking into flood as it rumbles
into Roseburg, barely keeping within
high-water markers, eager to escape
up its banks, visit the neighbors.

Setting sun shines it to molten silver—
for summer's sunsets it holds the rays
long into darkness, shining in its mold,
solid lump left behind, waiting to be
gathered and strung for Gaia's wearing.

# Fly-Fishing on the Rogue River

*Monty Cartwright*

The old fisherman stands alone, no anglers in sight.
Waist deep upstream from washboard ripples,
he relishes the taste of the Rogue's cool morning vapor.
Balancing himself atop mossy river rocks,
the Rogue's flow massages away arthritic knee pain.
Through film-coated eyes he studies the river's personality,
savoring hushed moments between decision and action.

He patiently begins the ritual dance of man and fish.
With a maestro's movement of his fly-rod,
he orchestrates the feathered insect along looped swirls,
positioning it to skim above percolating bubbles of slumbering steelhead.
Inner peace comes to the old man—time no longer exists, health problems
        disappear, regrets
are forgotten, decisions are put on hold.

Between an eye-blink and a swallow,
the floating fly is replaced by exploding water.
A rainbow flash is launched from the Rogue's depth.
He has seized his dance partner!

Fish and man embrace in a ballet of give and take.
Today the curtain-call belongs to him;
tomorrow the trout's pirouette may abruptly end their performance.
Regardless of the finality,
the old man is grateful for another day on the Rogue River—for solitude,
        reflection, and grace
time with a fish.

# The Little Heroine

## William Minshall

My grandaunt, Della A. (Watson) Montgomery (1876–1967), scaled Oregon's highest mountain twice in the 1890s. Some of my most pleasant childhood memories were of visits to my Aunt Della's home. Whenever entering her house, I would stop in the hallway to study a painting hanging on the wall that depicted a line of climbers approaching the top of a snow-covered mountain. She explained that it showed an actual party of climbers reaching the summit of Oregon's Mount Hood, and that the third figure below the summit, wearing a long ankle length skirt, was she. I loved to hear her recount the details of that climb, especially the part where she said, "I had to give up some of my dignity by dropping petticoats along the way to lighten the load."

Della's family had moved from Indiana to a farm in Hood River Valley. There, Della met the Langille family. Sarah Langille and her sons operated Cloud Cap Inn, and the boys loved exploring the peak and guiding climbers to the summit. In 1893, Doug and Will Langille invited Della, a young girl of just fifteen years, to join them on a climb to the top of the peak.

On August 10, 1893, the three climbers arose at 4:30 AM and were on the trail from the inn an hour later. They followed the route known as Wy'east, first climbing Cooper Spur, and then crossing the icy surface of Newton Clark Glacier to a long, high ridge leading to the summit. They stopped near the "hot rocks," where steam issues from the ridge, to eat lunch and send mirrored sun flashes back to the inn. As they reached the topmost point, they marveled at the breathtaking view in all directions, and then signed the summit register.

Their descent followed the same route they took coming up, and they had to take great care not to fall in the loose rocks and steep snow slopes. The tired group reached the inn by 4:30 PM. This climb marked only the second time a woman had climbed Mount Hood by that route. Greatly impressed with Della's efforts, Doug Langille composed a colorfully written account of the climb in which he refers to her as their "Little Heroine."

The following year, a group of Mount Hood climbers and hikers decided to organize a mountaineering club to be called the Mazamas. A charter climb was made on July 19, 1894, when 155 men and 38 women reached the summit. The Langilles invited Della to join the group of 22 who started at Cloud Cap Inn and ascended by the steep Cooper Spur route. Photographer C. C. Lewis also climbed with that group and managed to photograph the line of climbers just reaching the summit. An unknown artist made a water color painting based on that much-published photo—the same painting that used to hang on my Grandaunt Della's wall.

# Monet Landscape

*Sara Fox*

Before me lay sprawling sets of multicolored hills. Reds, oranges, yellows, purples, and blues made up the swirling patterns of color in the rock; my eyes were astonished. Even though the weather around me soared to a blistering 115 degrees, inside I sensed a feeling of cool tranquility as I looked upon this natural wonder: the Painted Hills, one of Oregon's striking native beauties.

The Painted Hills are one of the three sections of the John Day Fossil Beds National Monument, located in Wheeler County in central Oregon. My family and I were driving to Iowa that summer and stopping at all the parks or famous sights along the way. I remember the Painted Hills vividly, not just because of the heat, but also because of their splendor. Just being there, and looking at them, I felt like I had walked into a Monet painting.

# Dabbling

*Cheryl Garrett*

Come dabble your toes in the water with me,
at the beach, at the beach, by the open sea.
If your heart is weary and your soul is torn,
then upon the tides let your pain be borne.
Come wash away the sorrow you feel,
because only then can you know it's real.
If you have any doubts, the ocean knows,
and it's waiting for you to come dabble your toes.

# Alone

*Sharon Sargent*

A white swath of snow layers the environment. Trees, mountains, and sky are all the same color in different shades. I scan the horizon and lose myself in the stark vastness.

Somewhere behind me, my family is playing in the snow. They ride atop black tubes and launch themselves careening down steep slopes, laughing and whooping with excitement.

I wandered away from them, aching for isolation. The noise and people and industrial machinery of the Mount Hood ski park hold little attraction for my picky attention span. In place of them I discover the cool and seductive world of the mountain winter. It draws me in until there is nothing, empties me, and then fills me with peace.

Someone may be missing me. Or not. As I take in a breath of crisp and refreshingly cold air, concern fades to the back of my mind. I find myself alone, and yet happier than I ever am when surrounded by people.

# Our Feet Dangle

My first summer at Shakespeare Camp and I was scared, scared of messing up the entire production of *Two Gentlemen of Verona*. I played the part of Launce, a crazy, old man with a dog. I wasn't the only one who felt this nervous. Christy and Jennie felt the same. We were all scared, and the show would begin soon.

I had to calm down. Work all the nerves out. There was only one thing that could make me feel better about it all....

The beach. The ocean. The sunlight.

We walked down the road to the beach—Newport's own Nye Beach. We sat atop a cement cliff, and the sun was shining. We stared out at the beautiful view of Newport's sandy shores. None of us could believe we were only a few hours from our big performance. Anxious and nervous, the only thing we could do was breathe. Take in the salty air, feel the wind in our faces, feel gravity pull our feet down.

# Real Men

## *Andrew Harris*

Real men don't use trails. Real men don't use maps. Real men don't ask for directions. Real men know exactly where they are. Real men get lost. Unfortunately my hiking company consists entirely of real men. How else would a two-hour hike turn into a six-hour adventure?

We set out early in the morning, heading up into the hills by our campsite near Sisters. The Willamette National Wilderness lay ahead and somewhere in those tree-saturated hills a lake awaited us. Our mission: to find Upper Lake. Our hiking party consisted of my dad, my two uncles, and various men from my uncle's church. The day started out blistering, and gradually transformed into an inferno. As we hiked through the hills, arguments broke out among the leaders. One man's GPS said one thing; my uncle's said something different. This caused us to hike up, down, around, and over the same ridge. After wandering all around the congruent ridges, our party arrived at a lake. The men were overjoyed—we had reached our destination.

My uncle quietly approached me, making sure no one could hear us.

"This is the wrong lake," he said.

# Rain-Fed

*Barbara Houghton*

Oneonta's cooling creekside
Bridal Veil's icy thunder
Multnomah Falls cascading clear
Rain-washed wonder

Misty clouds white-shroud the cliffs
Raindrops glitter ferns
Mushrooms shod in dank fir bark
Devil's Punchbowl churns

Columbia River pushing west
Gorge-slicing power
Bonneville's turbines spinning out
Kilowatt hours

Not for us a dusty desert
Hot sandstone painted red
Our Northwest summers, cool and green
Are winter rainstorm fed.

# Lost in the Tides

## Taylor Richards

In the middle of summer, with the blue, cloudless sky overhead and the roaring ocean before me, I stood on Cannon Beach with the tides coming in to numb my feet. My black skimboard had been stabbed into the wet sand to keep it standing so that I didn't have to hold it up.

Something poked my shoulder.

I broke out of my trance and looked over at my best friend KK, who was grinning at me. She looked back over at the ocean, the wind whipping her hair across her face in all directions. She asked whether the tide was right yet, and I told her to wait just a little while longer. It was almost perfect.

The scent of the salt water burned in my nose. It was all I could smell, all I could taste, and the wind burned my eyes. With a sigh I told KK the tide was definitely right now, and it was time to go. When the next wave crashed onto the beach she pulled her board out of the sand and let the water wash over it to clean off the clumps of wet sand that stuck to the wax.

She stood, the board held in her hands and her stance wide, waiting for the water to retract back into the ocean, waiting for the perfect moment to steal a ride. I looked down the beach, making sure it was clear, and told her to go when the film of seawater was thin over the sand. She threw her board and it hit perfectly, gliding on the water. She sprinted after it, jumping onto it and gliding along with it.

Just from watching her I could feel the adrenaline dripping into my bloodstream, and it made my heart pound in my ribcage. When her board finally stopped, she jumped off and tried to pick it up quickly, but had some difficulty lifting it from the sand that held onto it like a starfish to the rocks. She ran back to me with her board under her arm and an exhilarated smile from ear to ear. I smiled back at her and started to laugh.

Now it was my turn. I picked up my board and washed it off as a huge wave hit the beach. It crawled towards us with cold fingers, hungry for the sand. The pressure of the water on my feet and legs was all I could feel; my entire body was completely numb. I waited for the perfect moment, my stance wide and my eyes focused on the strip of sand before me. I closed my eyes and exhaled heavily, and when I opened them I threw my board, ran beside it, and then jumped on it. I spread my arms out to help keep my balance and the feeling of weightlessness came over me. The board, the water, and the beach beneath me no longer existed. Adrenaline coursed through me and my heart raced. I glided down the beach, the water taking its time as it retreated back to the sea. It took me about forty-five seconds to stop, the gooey sand beginning to stick to the bottom of my board, and I hopped off, trying to pull it up. I tugged and pulled with all my strength but it would not come loose. I looked out to the ocean and a massive wave crashed onto the sand, depleting by small amounts as it charged toward me. I pulled harder and harder on the board, but it held to the sand.

The wave hit, the sheer force of it pushing me three steps back. Shivers ran down my spine as the water rose almost halfway to my knees. I heard KK trying to run toward me, wading through the water. I dove in, fully clothed except for shoes, and probed along the sand with my fingers, trying to find my board. The tide pushed and pulled me as it continued to wash back out to the sea, and a moment later I was above the surface, my sopping-wet hair in my face and my hands board-less.

That day I left the beach completely soaked to the bone, without a board, and somehow missing twenty dollars. Even though the beach is a great place to be in the summer, I don't think I've ever been as miserable. Oh well, I'll still be back next summer.

# Olallie Lake

*Nicholas Davis*

Fishing is one of the time-honored pastimes of the citizens of Oregon. One of the greatest fishing spots in this state is, without a doubt, Olallie Lake, which is filled in abundance with trout and salmon of only the most succulent variety. The lake lies in the shadow of Olallie Butte, a volcano famous for its pinnacles of magma-formed rock. An abandoned lookout tower sits at the top of this illustrious mountain, where it was once used to detect fires in the neighboring forests.

And what forests they were.

Whenever I went fishing with my father and uncle as a young boy, I would fantasize about exploring the forest next to the lake, and trying to see the many kinds of wildlife that supposedly lived there. Alas, I never saw hide nor tail of any such beast, but my father told me that this was because I lacked hunting skills.

He told me that, one day, he would take me hunting the wildlife with him. The catch, he told me, was that whatever I shot, I had to eat. My father did not believe in hunting for sport. He told me not to worry; it would be cooked in the comfort of my own home. He wasn't going to make me bite into raw flesh. I decided to remember to shoot only a deer when the time comes. I love venison.

I don't go to Olallie all that often anymore,
But I do intend to return someday;
Whether it be for the fish or for the deer,
Whether it be for the forest or for the volcano,
Whether it be for the fresh air or just to get away from it all,
And whether I go with my father or with my possible future son, so that
    he too can see the marvels of this beautiful site;
Whether it be for any of these reasons or for some other,
I do intend on coming back.
If only for one last time.

# An Experience at Skibowl

## Eric Peterson

It was just getting dark when I suited up to go snowboarding at Skibowl. Skibowl has the best night skiing runs, so I decided to go up to there instead of Mount Hood Meadows. I was so excited; my heart was pumping twice as fast from the adrenaline rush. My dad and brother were also getting ready to have an amazing night of skiing.

The snow was coming down slowly, but in big chunks, and it was just cold enough that I needed three layers on the top part of my body and four on my torso and legs. It was a perfect night for snowboarding—one of the best nights I've seen up at the mountain for a long time. As I walked with my dad and brother to get our lift tickets, we talked about what we thought the runs would be like, and we were very eager to go. We got to where we needed to be after about five minutes of walking, and I was already tired—it was a workout walking all that way in deep snow, and I was carrying my snowboard, which was quite heavy.

After I put my lift ticket on my jacket, I set my snowboard on the ground and strapped my left foot into the front binding; my brother did the same. We got to the first lift and waited in line until it was our turn to ride the lift. When we reached the top, we each sat down and strapped in the other foot; then we bombed down the mountain face.

My brother and I rode down that mountain run four or five times. Once we were done on that lift, we went to a couple of different runs before we went into the lobby to eat dinner with my dad. He told us about his time up at Skibowl, and my brother and I told him how it was going for us. We ate for about half an hour and then went back out to snowboard again. We stayed out for another two hours.

When we were done, we went back to the truck and I took off my snow pants, boots, and snow jacket to be more comfy. I got into the truck and poured myself some hot chocolate, but it wasn't very hot. I told myself it was just another amazing experience at Mount Hood, the best part of Oregon.

# Rafting the Clackamas River

*Andrew Schell*

It was a beautiful, sunny summer day in Oregon, with not a cloud in sight, a full tank of gas, and a packed car full of friends. We were all heading to Carver Park. With two rafts strapped to the top of the Suburban, we were an accident waiting to happen.

Although we were a freight train of teenagers, we were responsible enough to carry life jackets, and were not really doing anything out of the ordinary for a normal rafting trip. As Blake and Kyle were filling the rafts with air, Bryn, David, and I put on our shorts, and then switched with Blake and Kyle. Some of the others were putting sunblock on. Blake, Kyle, and I brought the coolers full of food and drinks down to the shoreline and waited to lift off on our journey.

As we pushed off the shore, there was a sense of freedom as I was sitting in the front of the raft with Blake behind me and a raft full of friends next to us. It was just supposed to be a relaxing trip, but we found ways to wreak havoc on each other. Whenever someone was leaning over the edge, we tried to boost him out of the boat. Somehow, one way or the other, we were going to make this trip epic.

The Clackamas River was the most extraordinary river that I had been on. Each rapid or turn in the river was a new and wonderful sight to see. As we made our way down the river, we found four or five rope swings. Some were better than others, but we pulled our rafts onto shore to go off the rope swings a few times and have some fun. As the warm summer day got hotter, we jumped into the water to cool off as we were floating down the river.

We made it to High Rocks, which meant that our trip was coming to an end soon, so we stopped off there and jumped off the rocks a few times to cool down and have some fun before eating lunch. We were having a blast. Once we left High Rocks, we saw cliffs of clay with beautiful colors;

it was definitely a sight that I remember to this day. When we made it to Clackamette Park, our trip was over. Several hours after we'd lifted off from Carver Park, we'd arrived at our destination. It was another wonderful summer day in Oregon.

# Multnomah Falls

*Philip Nguyen*

What comes to mind when someone mentions Oregon? Trees, scenic roads, the end of the Oregon Trail, the Portland Trail Blazers, and, of course, the rain. Well, these are some of the many things that come to me when I think of Oregon, my home state, where I was born and raised, and where it's almost always green.

Ever been to Oregon? If you have, have you ever heard of the falls that are the second-highest year-round waterfall in the nation? If you haven't, and you're looking for a hike that is worthwhile, then you should come to Multnomah Falls!

When I was little, my uncle used to take me to Multnomah Falls about once a year. Every time, I would stare in amazement at the falls. We would never make it to the top of the falls because I would always whine that my feet were hurting, so we always ended up turning around and going to eat some ice cream.

In my eighth-grade year, my team went on a field trip and took a school bus from Bonneville Dam to the falls. Before I could conquer the 1.2-mile hike to the top of the falls, I had to stop the growling in my stomach, so I decided it was time to eat my lunch. I started the hike a little bit later then some other people because I had eaten and they hadn't.

Starting the hike was very easy; continuing the hike was harder. On the way up I admired the view of the Columbia River. Every few minutes I would get to a higher point, and I would notice something new about the view of the gorge. About halfway through the hike, the sun came out and it started to get warm. This almost made me want to quit the hike. My feet were getting tired from the angled, paved trail going up towards the top of the falls, but it kept me going to hear people coming back down from the top calling "You're almost there!"

Finally, I made it to the top. The view of the Columbia Gorge was amazing. My only disappointment was that I did not have a camera to take a picture of it. Then it was time to go, so I started the 1.2-mile hike back down.

# Just Squeeze

*Melinda Jacobs*

Hunting season is exciting, and most hunters share the same joy. Hunters love to hunt. I had all the necessary items needed for hunting ready, knowing that when I woke up it would be opening day.

I tossed and turned all night long. My thoughts were racing. Was I ready for the hunting season? Would I successfully tag a buck? The alarm clock finally sounded off; it was time to get up. I sprang out of bed, turned the alarm off, jumped into my clothes, and rocketed down the stairs. I started the coffee brewing, and breakfast was on its heels. My gear was by the door. I was ready to go. My thoughts were still racing. Would I see a buck? Would I shoot a buck? One thing to remember: just squeeze.

Daylight was approaching, and we soon would be at our location. We had made arrangements to hunt on private property. With a month to hunt deer, private property was a first choice; public lands are harder to hunt. This place was nearby, thirty minutes away. It looked like we had good timing. It was just daylight, and we could see to shoot. We parked. Quietly, I got out. I made sure not to make too much noise. I had my rifle, and I was ready to go. One more sip of coffee, and I shut the door. We locked the pickup and headed for the gate. My thoughts were still racing. What do I do when I get one? I would have help. I had to shoot one first. I had to remember: just squeeze.

We entered through the gate. I jacked a shell in my rifle and clicked the safety on. Our plans were to hunt up the ridge and wait at the top. There were four hunters. Two went up the open side and two went up through the brush to the ridge. Up the ridge we hunted. It was a clear October morning, but I could only see brush. October mornings in Oregon are cool, but the temperature can be real warm later in the day. We continued hunting up the ridge, picking our way though the bushes. We stopped in places to look things over. Perhaps we would see a buck on the way up. This ridge was hard to climb, harder since I was trying to hunt, too. I began to get warm, so I took my sweatshirt off and tied it around my waist. The climbing wasn't over. We followed deer trails, picking our way up, until we finally made it to the top of that ridge. We could see better, but there was still a valley and a small ridge before we'd be at the tip-top. My thoughts were back, and I had to remember to just squeeze. Don't jerk, just squeeze.

We headed down the little valley. It was a welcome trail; going down helped us to rest. We hadn't heard any shots, so no one had seen a buck yet. One small climb and we would be at the top. We climbed and crawled though the poison oak thickets. All the while, branches smacked me in the face and blackberry vines tried to trip me. I managed to find a small place to look around. The climb was like running a one-hundred-yard dash. I wanted to rest again, but there, across the hill, I spotted a deer.

I drew up on the deer, clicked my safety off, and noticed right away it was a buck. I found a place to lie down and looked to make sure he was legal. He was. The buck was a forked-horn. I was exhausted from the climb, but amazingly, I wasn't shaking. I was too tired. I took aim and my thoughts raced. I had to focus; *just squeeze*. With my crosshairs on his head, where I wanted the bullet to go, I squeezed the trigger. He dropped out of sight.

"Did I get him?" I asked.

"You got him! You got him! He'll be lying right over there. You got your first buck! Way to go!"

We made our way over to the buck, and there he lay. With one shot from my Ruger 243, I had my first buck, a forked-horn. Now I was ready for more instruction.

I've learned, and I'm still learning, about hunting. I enjoy hunting in Oregon. My thoughts aren't racing so much now. I squeezed. Just squeeze.

# Cascade Head

*Carol A. Hayes*

The narrow gravel road winds up and away from the highway, through tall timber and shadows that come together above the road. Through the open car window, the clean smell of fir and moss begins to work its magic on my soul. Here and there birds flit through slanting sun; their wings are jewels, as is their song.

Free at last from the confines of the car, the trail beckons me forward. I walk silently up the path to hear the peace, to absorb the vitality of the very air. Subtly upward the trail goes, through salal and alder. A great hollow tree with moist and dewy ferns inside marks a crossroad. The path directly ahead seems to take me with it, up, ever up. My mind clears and empties with the total feeling of walking and breathing, walking and breathing. Stairs fashioned from logs and earth rise steeply up the hillside. Vine maple whispers to me as I pass. The air cools. Suddenly I step out of the forest into a sea of grass, chest-high, that moves in waves that rasp and rustle against my parka. The wind whips tears into my eyes; my hands are numb. Gradually the height of the grass decreases and the trail becomes a mere track through the restless land-sea. I am at the top of the world, and I am held transfixed. Far below lies the great Pacific, blue and limitless, wrapping itself around the rocky headlands, caressing the beaches with white foam that speaks of crashing sounds I cannot hear. The sky is around me, mountain wraiths of fog suddenly enfold me, and I am closer to the sky than to the sea.

As I walk in this place, my personhood drops away. I am not mother or daughter, sister or wife; I am neither young nor old. I am alive as the grasses are alive, as the sea is alive, as the very mountain is alive. I am as much an essence as the wind that strips me of my everyday reality and lifts me high above human entanglements. I belong upon this earth, and through its splendid beauty I am free.

# Learning to Love the Sky

## Mary Emerick

I grew up in the forest. Slender-trunked, second-growth, the aftermath of years of logging, but forest nonetheless, dark inside, quiet, still.

When I came to Steens Mountain in eastern Oregon, I was afraid. A towering fault block, pushed up by geologic and volcanic forces, it stretched out under a big sky. Juniper and aspen clustered at lower elevations, but where I walked there was no place to hide.

Thunderstorms swooped in, lightning bouncing off the rocky cliffs above Little Wildhorse Lake. When it was clear, the sun burned down with what felt like ferocity. Sometimes great pillowy clouds wafted by, almost close enough to touch.

It felt dangerous to be so exposed, just me and my shadow crossing Kiger Gorge rim. In the evenings when I camped, I looked for my old friends, the trees. Everything felt stark and exposed. I wasn't sure I liked it much. I sat in camp, staring out at the view: multi-dimensional shades of brown and green, cliffs and ridges and flats all the way to the Nevada line. In the morning I donned my armor: sunscreen, floppy hat, map.

I'm not sure when I began to love the sky. Maybe it was my second summer in the Steens, mincing along a knife-edge between two deep gorges. The ground dropped off below my feet, the U-shaped valleys curving like bellies, a faint scattering of aspens near the rivers. Maybe it was my first winter, skiing up the snowed-in road, sun sparkling off a landscape turned white. Or maybe it was later than that, after I left for a misty rainforest, where sky was hard to find.

Now, far away from the Steens, I search for the sky. I push through thick stinging nettle and brush, trying to get high enough to reach the timberline. Somehow, though, it is never as big, as wild, as it was back on Steens Mountain. The sky is a smaller slice, the thunderstorms not as dramatic. I am never such a small figure as I was then, captivated and humbled by sky.

**Young Oregon**

*Young Oregon shows what it is like growing up in Oregon, with nostalgic stories of past experiences and pieces by young writers.*

# Dearest Oregon, Happy Birthday

## Tyler Nelson

Dearest Oregon,

I will start by wishing you the best on your 150th birthday. Hopefully you have received everything you put on your birthday list. I'm sorry I didn't get you anything this year, but I'm running low on cash, mostly because I've gone snowboarding so much. On that note, I believe a thanks is in order for all the great snowboarding.

Even with all the new snow, I'm glad it is now spring. I rather enjoy the sweet scent of your freshly sprouted buds. And spring means that summer is coming! I will be leaving you for about three weeks in the summer, as it is my family's tradition to visit my grandparents in Arizona every June. I must say I will miss you during this time, because it is considerably hotter there. Everything has to be done indoors or at an aquatic park. Your summers, beloved Oregon, are the best I have ever known. It's hot, but not too hot. I wish you could stay in the blissful summer stage forever, because your other seasons can be a tad dreary for my taste.

Also, summer is when strawberries are in season! There are not enough words of praise in the English dictionary to describe how divine your strawberries are. It is a practice in my household to go out early in the season and hand-pick the top berries we can find. We get baskets and baskets of those wondrous little fruits of yours. Your strawberries remind me that there is a God out there who loves us, because otherwise how would mankind be graced with such a gift as strawberries?

Another thing that I adore so much about you is your great outdoors. So many of my fondest childhood memories take place beneath your towering fir trees around a campfire. Now that I'm older, I still enjoy camping with my friends. This summer I am planning on bringing my friend Adam to the Redwoods with me. Last time we went to Lost Lake and paddled out to the middle for a view of your glorious Mount Hood.

Again, I wish you the best, and a very happy 150th. May your trees stay tall and your strawberries grow aplenty.

Faithfully,

Tyler Nelson

# Summer Days

*Kayla Livesay*

During the summer, my backyard was where I stayed for all hours of the day. To me, there was no greater place. It had a swing set, a trampoline, a sandbox, and a little pool with a slide. My sister and I would be outside for hours at a time playing in our backyard, and she was always the first to go inside. As we got older, I was still the one who was constantly outside. Now I realize that the reason why I loved our backyard so much was because of the weather and the life around me. During a typical Oregon summer, our backyard was filled to the brim with flowers, bushes, trees full of leaves, and soft green grass. The heat never got so hot that you couldn't stand to be outside, and there was always a light breeze or bit of shade coming from our giant oak and maple trees. You could always hear our neighbors out and about in their own yards. Some would be mowing their lawns, while others would be having barbeques with their families, and others would be out playing with their children.

Now, Oregon is known for rain, but there is no comparison to summer rain. When it rains and the sun is still out, there is nothing that looks more beautiful. The strong scent of cut grass, sweet rain, and heat from the sun are enough to make anyone go insane with happiness. Hearing that summer rain pattering softly on my roof and windows would make me fall asleep in an instant, and it still does. The only time to really see, understand, and appreciate Oregon is in its breathtaking summertime, when you will see Oregon's inhabitants at their happiest.

# The Crater State

## Ben Roebber

amily vacations will make a young mind run rampant. When I was six, or maybe seven, years old my family took a trip to Crater Lake. That week, we stayed on the lake's campground with some family from California. Seeing the lake (but more importantly, the crater) for the first time, I imagined titanic dinosaurs struggling in front of the monolithic volcano that formed the crater millions of years ago.

In my dream world, the volcano would engorge with lava, rising, heaving until—*boom!* It exploded, sending an earth-shattering cataclysm throughout the land. Where once there was a majestic mountain, there was now only a molten, smoking crater.

After thousands of years, Oregon rain and snowmelt filled up the prodigious hole, forming the 1,943-foot-deep tourist attraction that we've all come to recognize as a state icon. Just the sight of such a fantastic gouge on the Earth's surface made my imagination explode like Mount Mazama itself. The experience left a crater on my impressionable mind.

# Playing in the Rain

*Terra McClellan*

Walking home from school one day in the third grade, my sister and I jumped into the deep rain puddles, splashing dirty water all over our clothes and giggling. Oregon was the perfect place for me; I loved the rain. I *adored* it. I had always found the rain to be soothing, the sound of it as it hit the ground and splattered into a hundred tiny water droplets was calming, and the cool liquid feel of it against my skin was heaven.

My grandmother scolded us for being so wet when we arrived on her doorstep, warning us that we would catch cold unless we came inside and got warmed up and changed our clothes. I grinned, young and careless of my health. I sat on her stairs and stared out of the grimy window as I removed my shoes and socks. The gray, cloudy skies and the soft torrents of rain that came down to meet with hard pavement took my breath away with their beauty. Suddenly, I longed to go outside and play in the rain again.

I stood up and glanced down the hall; my grandmother was busy helping my younger sister out of her wet clothes. With a sneaky smile, I opened the front door quietly, stepped out onto the porch, and shut it behind me. I ran out into the middle of the parking lot and jumped, with my bare feet, into the largest puddle, laughing loudly in the silence. I could hear the distant splash of cars driving down McLoughlin. I spread my arms and spun around, dancing all by myself in the rain, loving the feel of it washing over my skin, until my grandmother noticed I was missing. She ushered me inside and promptly gave me a spanking with the wooden paddle. As I stood in the corner for the next ten minutes, I could still feel the giddy aftereffects of my dance in the rain. It had *so* been worth it.

I woke up the next day with a sniffly nose and a sore throat.

# The 2008 Snow

*Gus McD*

My first memory of the 2008 snow, the most snow Oregon has seen in forty years, was my dad jerking the covers off me and saying, "Get up, boy!" He always makes the small and mundane things in life exciting. Sometimes I think he never really grew up; he can be like a kid in a candy store on a daily basis. His energy level is off the chart. He had already been up and had come in to get me to come out and go on an adventure. He was ready to build an igloo or have a snowball war. I don't really remember which he wanted to do first. The next thing I knew he was opening all the cupboards in my room, and I said, "What are you looking for?" He answered, "Your binoculars. There is a giant Golden Eagle out the window, and I want to get a closer look!"

The other thing I really noticed was how quiet everything is when the snow is so deep. It's like the world is holding its breath waiting to see what's next. Snow can present challenges that rain does not. Like we were stranded and had to ride a four-wheeler to the top of our driveway to get out; I thought that was pretty cool. It was a little awkward trying to carry Christmas presents on the front of the four-wheeler.

Four-wheelers can come in handy when you need them. I rode to my cousin's house, and from there we rode clear to Canby. What a thrill! No cops in sight, the wind in your face, and the snow flying behind you. This is a memory of Oregon I won't soon forget. Oregon is the best place to live.

# Fond Memories of Those Tragic Years

*Harriet Beulah Smith Guardino*

In the early 1930s, there was no state or federal aid for farmers, no welfare, no Social Security. My parents owned a small dairy farm in Grants Pass. As the Great Depression engulfed the nation, the long hours of hard work with very little rest and worry over a dwindling income took their toll on my family. My mother, Catherine Elizabeth Ferguson Dobbie Smith, finally collapsed from sheer nervous exhaustion.

And so my father, John Reynolds Smith, was forced to sell the farm. With the money from this sale, he chose to make his last stand on the Croxton Ranch, a two-hundred-acre spread of dry land on Louse Creek, about five miles north of Grants Pass. I remember the day we drove our small herd of cattle on foot down the back roads of town, across the highway, and onto a lightly used dirt trail that meandered through the wooded hills to our destination. I felt like a pioneer.

For my mother, moving into an old two-story frame house—which boasted a real brick fireplace but no plumbing—meant even more hard work. But to me it was exciting and romantic. I didn't really know we were poor, since everyone around us was in similar straits.

As a sixth grader in a new school district, I was eager to make new friends. Oak Grove School was located in a wooded area about a mile and a half from our place. It was a one-room grammar school that housed all eight grades under the tutorage of one teacher, Miss Dorothy Jones (who, incidentally, was also the janitor). The "Bug House," as we affectionately dubbed the school, was very primitive. Kerosene lamps hung on the walls. A water bucket, set on a shelf in the cloakroom, had one dipper from which we all drank. A wood stove, converted from an empty oil drum, stood against the front wall near the teacher's desk. Four rows of desks—one size to fit all—completed the furnishings. Two outdoor privies, positioned on the far corners of the property, were equipped with the standard tissue of the day—a Sears catalog.

Playground equipment consisted of a couple of rusty swings and a broken-down teeter-totter, half of an old baseball bat, and a ball that was unraveling at the seams. Sometimes we brought our own toys from home to play with—like dolls, cars, or marbles. At recess we vented our energy running races and playing games like Annie Over, London Bridge, cops and robbers, and tag.

Patched overalls and darned socks were standard apparel, and flour sack underwear was as kosher as spit curls and the "shingle bob." A few children came to school barefoot, unable to afford shoes. Getting a new pair of shoes was a big event, and you wore them until the heels were worn down and the soles flapping. I remember walking to school in my father's boots on rainy days because I didn't have a pair of my own.

Although we always had enough to eat, food was scarce in a lot of homes. There were stories of men who took potato peelings to work in their lunch pails. A friend of mine told me about the time her father thought she was peeling away too much potato and made her go back and peel the peelings. You simply couldn't afford to waste anything in those days.

Month by month, my father watched his life's savings melt away. The second year at Louse Creek was especially hard. The dry ground didn't yield enough to make a living. Near Christmas my horse, Dollie, who was used for both plowing and riding, died from some strange malady. My parents tried to save her by administering homemade enemas, but she bolted to her feet and began to run. She ran until she collapsed and died. That dampened the holiday spirit considerably. On top of that, there was almost nothing under the Christmas tree except for a couple of packages from a total stranger that were bluntly marked, "To some poor little girls." However, my attention fell on a brightly wrapped gift, to me from my older sister Virginia ("Ginna"). What could it be? I felt it and shook it, trying to guess what was inside. My mother and sister sat nearby, not saying a word, but their sly smiles portended mischief. Eagerly, I tore open the wrappings and found, to my complete dismay, a dried-out "horse biscuit" with a note that read: "Sorry. I got you another horse for Christmas, but it ran away." I laugh about it now, but at the time I failed to see the humor, and furiously threw the open package at my giggling sister.

Folks had to be resourceful to withstand the onslaught of the Depression. Somehow, my parents never seemed to lose faith, not even when the winter temperatures fell below zero and one of their valuable heifers died while calving. Shortly after that, another plow horse, old Bessie, died from exposure. It was so cold that winter that the creek froze over two inches thick. But my father, in his usual fashion, turned tragedy into triumph. He went down to the creek with an axe, a pick, and a wheelbarrow, and loaded the wheelbarrow with ice to bring back to the house. Meanwhile, my mother hunted out the ice cream freezer and filled it with enough batter to make two quarts of ice cream. Ginna and I took turns churning, and when the ice cream was frozen the four of us gathered around a blazing fire, wrapped up in our heavy winter coats, and enjoyed every luscious bite.

Finally, in the spring, the folks' money ran out. My sister moved in with a family in town to work for board and room while she attended high school. Mother took a housekeeping job to help support the family. She made five dollars a week in addition to her board and room, with a few hours off on Sundays, and no holidays. When school was out, my father and I moved to town as well.

It was tough, but we made it! And what amazes me is the fact that some of my fondest memories have come out of those tragic years.

Mark E. Walton

There is no better feeling than being back home in Oregon. I first left Oregon in 1972; in that time, I have been to sixteen countries and forty-nine of the fifty states. Out of all the places I have been, Oregon is the best place to be. The weather is great, and geographically the state has everything from the ocean to the desert with great mountains and green valleys. My travels within the state have taken me every place except the Steens Mountains. As for my favorite part of the state, that is the north-eastern section, especially the Wallowas.

I was born in Roseburg at the old Mercy Hospital in 1954. I do remember the big blast of 1959 because we lived close enough to the downtown area that our house shook, and all the blinds fell down. My father, who worked for the telephone company and was a volunteer fireman, had to rush into town only to find that his best friend, the Roseburg fire chief, had died trying to save everyone. When I was halfway through first grade, we moved to Florence, and that is where I grew up and graduated from Siuslaw High School.

Growing up in Florence was great! This was during the '60s and '70s, when there were twenty-eight lumber mills within a twenty-five mile radius of Florence, along with commercial fishing; the town was growing and thriving. We survived the Columbus Day Storm, the tidal wave of '64, the record snowfall of February '69 (three feet of snow), and the exploding whale (we were on the dune watching the spectacle). We fished, clammed, crabbed, hunted, and grew vegetables that we canned for later use.

As kids, we were always busy with playing in the woods and the sand dunes, swimming at Honeyman State Park, beachcombing, running, and growing up in a safe and healthy environment. I would not trade my childhood for anything.

To this day, I am still in contact with many of the people I grew up with. And what is amazing is that I encounter even more of these people in my travels around the state.

# Mabel's Journal

*Alison Mae Lasher*

*A short story by Alison, age ten, inspired by the diaries of her great-grandmother's aunt, Mabel F. O'Brian, who immigrated to Oregon in 1892.*

FEBRUARY 12, 1892
LEON, KANSAS
Dear Journal,
Pa got home from Oregon. It's a wonderful land. Ma said, "I suppose we have to pack. We're going west." I'm excited to go on a trip, but I am glum because I will leave my friends. Pa said that we leave on Tuesday. I hope Tuesday never comes.

FEBRUARY 16
Today we leave for Abilene. Now I am in the back of the wagon.

FEBRUARY 23
ON THE TRAIN
Riding a train sounded like fun. It was for the first half hour. After that it has been boring. I packed my needlepoint bag. I'm just learning, and I'm going to make a pillow cover for Pa's rocking chair.

FEBRUARY 24
CROSSING THE GREAT PLAINS
The train has a steam engine; a baggage car where our trunks, boxes, Pa's rocking chair and Ma's organ are; a mail car; a tourist car for sleeping; and our coach with forty seats. The land is unbelievably *dull*—a flat, grassy plain. No trees anywhere! We stopped for wood and water for the steam engine.

FEBRUARY 26

ROCKY MOUNTAINS

I was just getting used to the switchbacks when the train stopped. There was a small avalanche on the tracks. Pa, Robert, and Joe helped shovel snow.

FEBRUARY 28

ROCKY MOUNTAINS

I have nothing to write about. Every day is the same. My back hurts from sleeping sitting upright. Breakfast is cold again. Jenny is crying and Milton is teasing Ida Belle and Eveline. There is nothing to see outside except snow and sometimes a dead tree. *Leap year! Tomorrow is February 29!*

MARCH 1,

SALT LAKE CITY, UTAH TERRITORY

We can't go any further on this train. We have three choices: Virginia City, where they found gold, or California, where they found gold, or Oregon.

MARCH 3

BOISE, IDAHO

I didn't write yesterday. Everything is the same. We've been on a train for eight day and nights. Pa sent a telegram in Morse code from Boise. We will be at The Dalles on Sunday.

MARCH 4

BAKER CITY, OREGON

The land was flat along the Snake River. We just crossed the river. We are going up a hill with lots of small switchbacks and a *huge* one. Baker City has many modern buildings; Pa thinks it has too many saloons to raise children.

MARCH 5
THE DALLES, OREGON

I woke up and saw the biggest river ever. Pa calls it the Columbia River. This is our last day on the train.

MARCH 6, 1892
DUFUR, OREGON

The first day in our new house! Yesterday we got off the train in The Dalles. Pa's friend was waiting with Pa's wagon. We rode to Dufur. Then we rode five miles to the house Pa built in Rail Hollow. The scenery is grass and hills. The house is in the valley. March 10th is my birthday. I will be thirteen!

# South Beach Jetty

*Skylar Mathew Morris*

When I was a young boy, I used to venture down to the South Jetty at South Beach State Park, imagining joyous times, riding my bike with music blaring in my ears from my headphones. I lived in a small house that was infested with all sorts of nasty critters; this became my castle, my playground. I would never have had such a great time if not for the luscious, green, milky sea that became my backyard. I would swim, run on the golden-brown beach, and when the day was almost done, I would do a little crabbing to catch Red Rock Crab.

The Yaquina Bay was just ten steps south. Day after day I would watch the crabbing boats. When I reached the age of twelve, I would head down the jetty and catch lingcod. This saved money for me and Mom; I would catch fish, clean them, and package them up with a friend who owned a dive shop near where I lived. In this way I was able to catch and freeze many lingcod and have supper for many nights to come. I will never forget the South Beach Jetty of the Oregon coast.

# Rain on a Friday Night

*JD Bricker*

Every Friday night in the fall at high schools across the state, dreams are alive as football teams take the field. Parkrose is no different. The Parkrose football team is not known for winning, but that's not the point. My favorite thing about Oregon is playing football in the pouring rain. Nothing compares to the feeling of being under the lights and having that rain rolling off your helmet. I am on my way to college to play football in another state, but nothing will ever compare to playing in the Oregon rain.

## Forrest Murphy

Bigfoot: lurker of the Oregon wilderness, or legend? Some say that he's a myth the Native Americans made up to keep their children from wandering. The Himalayans call him "Yeti" and say he's a monster who eats people who venture too far up the mountain. In my mind, he's a giant creature who just wants to be left alone.

I was going on a camping trip up high in the northwest, near the mountains, with my friend Zoe, whom I've known since I was born; her dad, whom I've also known since birth; and his wife, who was Zoe's stepmom. As we were leaving I remember thinking, "Something about this trip is going to be weird," which was spot on, because it was *weird*.

We arrived at the campsite about three hours later. We got there at around 7 PM and unpacked as soon as we got there. We roasted weenies on sticks (I had four) and then we had s'mores. I went to bed full and satisfied. We all woke up around 9 AM, and guess what we ate? Weenies! We all went on a hike after that. It was only a two-mile hike, but we saw a lot of wildlife. When we returned to the campsite around 12 PM, we all went for a swim for a few hours. After that I felt ill, so I went to bed around 6 PM That's when things got weird.

I woke up around midnight, and went about forty feet out of the campground to use the bathroom. I was heading back toward the camp when I heard a rustling in the bushes. Being the lil' adventurer I was, and am today, I went toward the sound. It stopped. I said "Hello?"…and then it ran. It ran away from me, and I saw the top of its head and legs. It was about nine feet tall, and it must've been running sixty miles per hour. I only glimpsed it. Freaked out as heck, I went back to bed and told the others about it in the morning. Then we packed up and left.

I knew it was Bigfoot. I don't think it saw me, but I was still scared. I'm almost grateful I didn't see its face—I probably would've passed out. We got home and I told my family. It was one of the coolest things that's ever happened to me.

Some people say Bigfoot is a myth. They are wrong.

# Bethel Elementary School, Salem, Oregon—A Historic Farm-Family Community

*Kitri McGuire*

When we were in grade school, my little brother Alex and I constantly (but unsuccessfully) tried to convince our parents to let us walk the half-mile to school from our house. It was the 1980s, and there was no need for us to walk along busy State Street, a few miles east of Salem, Oregon, since a bus picked us up every morning at the end of 59th Avenue and shipped us the short distance east to Bethel Elementary School.

Like everyone at Bethel, we looked forward to school. Located next to Kuenzi Turf & Nursery, the school building was surrounded by acres of fields. The playground was complete with four-square courts painted on the blacktop, three huge tractor tires to climb on, and evergreen trees to gather under. Bethel was a family community where only three teachers taught. Outdoor school was the highlight of every year, and the playground monitor had the final say in any dispute.

We were not the first generation to pass through Bethel School. In the mid-1800s, the location was surrounded by timberland, and a sawmill owned by Dan Early was operated on the site. When the local timber supply ran out, the sawmill was torn down, and Early donated the property to the Dunkard Brethren, who built Bethel Church in the sawmill's place. Local farming families could choose to send their children to the contribution-supported school the church maintained, but as time passed, several leading families of the church moved away and the remaining families could not maintain both the church and the school. The vacant church was sold and became Bethel School in 1903.

The school building that exists now was built in 1925 and employed one teacher for eight grades of students. A second teacher was added in 1955, and ten years later the school changed from eight grades to six, forcing local families with seventh and eighth graders to pay tuition for their children to attend Parrish Junior High in downtown Salem.

When my brother and I attended Bethel, there were three classrooms for the sixty-five students who attended: one in the basement for the first and second grades, one on the main floor for the third and fourth, and a portable building outside for the fifth and sixth. Our music classes were taught in the library, formerly the one main classroom, where a stovepipe hole was still visible in the ceiling.

Today, Bethel Elementary School still houses three classrooms, but the class format has changed again, dropping from six grades to three. Kindergarteners through second graders attend Fruitland Elementary two miles away, and the third through fifth graders attend Bethel. Although part of the basement has been converted to a computer lab, not much else has changed. The farm-family tradition of Bethel Elementary School continues, and some of my former classmates are now sending their own children to Bethel. My mother currently teaches fourth grade in the basement classroom. To this day, she still doesn't let her students walk to school.

# Mighty

*Anna Zekan*

"**S**o is this what you kids listen to these days?" asked my father, attempting to connect with his moody teenage daughter. I didn't answer, just glanced at the clock. Only six more hours, I thought. I didn't try to hide my boredom as I sat beside my gruff father on our drive across Oregon to visit my older brother, who was attending college in Walla Walla, Washington.

I gaped as I laid eyes on the magnificent walls of the Columbia for the first time. I changed the song to fit the mood—The Stones' "Wild Horses"—and my father actually complimented my music taste, for once. The hazy, yellow hills of desolate Interstate 84 contrasted with the hustle and bustle of Portland. My father and I agreed that the vast, deep blue river, peppered with occasional windsurfers, was a sight to behold. He and I chatted and joked; something about the unbelievable sight set the stage for a kind of family bonding I didn't know could exist. At that moment I realized how much I had taken Oregon's beauty for granted. I owe my family relations to one of our great state's strongest features—the mighty Columbia.

# Life on the Willamette

*Jackie Heifner*

Springtime brings back memories of the hog lines on the Willamette: getting up in the morning while it was still pitch black so we could find the best spot to anchor. Packing the cooler and the herring. The smell of two-stroke oil as the motor started up. My dad negotiating the river by feel because he knew every nook and cranny. Throwing the anchor off the bow and letting the boat glide into position. Rigging the poles with the coveted herring and giving it just the special touch of anise oil or WD-40. Sitting patiently and nervously waiting for the bite. Hours of reading, playing cribbage, or just watching the birds and other fishermen. Pulling anchor when the tugs would blow their horns to enter the mouth of the Clackamas. Setting the hook and yelling "Fish on!" Floating down river to net my fish. Feeling proud as could be because I was a girl and I could rig my line, set my hook, and catch my own fish. A thirty-pound Chinook for dinner. Better yet, my dad's smokehouse, filled with salmon and applewood so everyone could smell the wonderful aroma and anticipate the final product.

I am a third-generation Oregonian. To this day, every time I cross the river over the old bridge in Oregon City or by I-205, I still take a peek over the side to see how many boats are out, and if there are any floating free to net their fish. I love the fact that wild salmon make their journey back to their origins every season like clockwork. Even though the runs and regulations have changed in the forty years since I started fishing, there will always be the allure of the natural and wild process that takes place in the spring. The river is part of my soul. I hope the future generations of Oregonians will be able to keep this memory alive, and preserve the rivers for the fish, the beauty, and the recreational opportunities that we all love about this great place called Oregon.

# Summer of '96

*Tianna Munoz*

I will always remember my grandma sending my brothers and me out to the fields to pick blackberries for her famous blackberry ice cream in the summer of '96. It all started when my oldest brother, Gabe, was annoying my grandma, so she sent all three of us kids out to get the blackberries.

We went behind a fence, and there were thousands of blackberry bushes. We walked through the path of the blackberries in a line: my brother Byron, me in the middle, and then Gabe behind me. Byron noticed a huge beehive by one of the bushes with a lot of blackberries on it, so he decided to start throwing rocks at it. Then I joined him, because I just wanted to hurry up and get the berries and leave.

After I joined Byron, Gabe decided to start throwing rocks too, and all of a sudden, bees started swarming us. Byron started yelling at Gabe to run, but Gabe just stood there and continued to throw rocks at the hive. Bees started to cover my brothers, but for some strange reason they weren't attacking me. It seemed like time was standing still while my brothers were fighting off the bees. Seconds later, reality came back and my brothers were pulling and pushing me to get out of the spot where they were being attacked.

As we ran back to my grandparents' house, I remember smiling because the bees hadn't attacked me; but, instead of smiling, my brothers were calling each other names, because Gabe wanted to continue to throw things and Byron wanted to get out of there un-stung. As soon as we got to the back door, my grandma came running out because she saw the boys bleeding all over, so she asked us what had happened. As we told her, she began taking the stingers out of their ears, cheeks, legs, and arms. She then asked me how come I hadn't been stung, and I couldn't really explain it to her.

# Outdoor School

*Lizzie Poetzsch*

"Girls! Get up!" my counselor yelled. I remember thinking that it couldn't be time to get up already; I had just fallen asleep. Sure enough, it was time to get up and go down to breakfast. Then it would be time for our daily learning experience. We were going on a hike to the forest, all the way to the top of the not-so-large mountain, and man, was I excited.

My cabin group quickly finished breakfast and headed out to the flagpole for the flag-raising. Then Buckwheat, a counselor, called over my cabin group and a few others who were going to the forest that day. He told us to follow him and to listen to all the other counselors who were going to be assisting us. Then, up we went.

"Oh, my gosh, I'm going to die," I told my friend when we were halfway up. She was concentrating and mumbled something about how it was going to be worth it when we got to the top. Right at that moment, I felt like I would have liked nothing better than to sit down right there and rest, but Flavor Flav, our group's leader, was on a roll and was more interested in jogging to the top so he could see his girlfriend for lunch. I was complaining about how I was going to push Flavor Flav off the cliff if he didn't let us take a break in the next two minutes, when we finally reached the top.

It was one of the most beautiful things I've ever seen. You could see the beach and all the rocks and the sky. The sky was an amazing color of darkish light blue. I was so happy that Flavor Flav hadn't let us take a break, because that totally would have wasted the time all my friends and I spent together, eating lunch and watching for whales, playing lemonade and singing songs at the top of our lungs. Most of all, though, just being able to share that moment with every single one of my best friends was a miracle on its own.

I had a lot of fun at outdoor school. Considering all the events that took place, this one was by far my favorite. I hope that I will never forget it, because I learned that not everything is handed to you. Sometimes you have to work for something wonderful, and let me tell you, did I work hard to get up that mountain. Coming down, however—well, that's a different story.

# Jeff Lovelady

I am the first Oregon native born in my family. My dad is from Southern California and moved here in the '70s on a crazy hunch that he would find better jobs up here, because he was running out of work in California. My mom is from Washington and moved here with her family when she was a kid.

When he came here, my dad loved to go out and party and go to bars with his new friends. It's very weird to think that my dad, in his prime, went out and partied like crazy. If you think about your parents having a life before you, it will blow your mind. They actually didn't come straight home from work on Friday night and start making dinner—they got dressed up and went out to party. My mom told me these wild stories about how she and my dad would go on exciting dates in Portland.

The craziest story my dad told me was about the time when he was going out to the bar on his new Harley and a bee flew into his helmet. He couldn't get the bee out. A cop pulled him over because he thought that he had been drinking, which was funny because he was headed to a bar. When my dad pulled over, he jumped off his bike and ripped off his helmet. The cop freaked out and thought he was going to attack him, so he drew his gun. After everything simmered down, my dad continued on his journey to get his party on.

If you ever have the chance, I would highly recommend that you ask your parents about how they partied and how they met. But, for your sake, beg them to spare you certain details. Trust me, this will help keep away the too-much-information part.

# Champions

*Landon Martinez*

I looked up at the scoreboard in disbelief. My knees were weak and my head was spinning. I had just been drilled by Lake Oswego's middle linebacker. With less than two minutes left in the game, and being down 12–14, we had to score quickly. I got up, shook my head, and gathered myself. We were on our own forty-five-yard line. The clock was ticking. No time for a huddle.

We quickly set up in our "spread offense" as I barked out the play. "Green 23, Green 23!" I called. That's where the wide-out runs a slant as the slot runs an "out" rout. I called the cadence and got the ball. I quickly scanned the field and threw to my open receiver. Incomplete. I couldn't believe it. The clock was stopped so the team huddled up and I went to the coach to get the play.

"I want the ball," I told him, and he nodded as if to say, "It's up to you then." On fourth and long you don't really have a lot of options for plays to run. The defense expected a long pass down the sideline to get a first down and get out of bounds quickly to stop the clock.

Our coach knew this. He looked at me and said, "Are you sure you can do this? Are you sure you want the ball? If we don't convert, game's over."

"Yes, coach." I answered definitively.

The play was "Pop Bottles." That's where we motion our running back out to receiver to draw the middle linebacker out, to open up the middle for me to run through. This time we were keeping our back in to block.

This was it. Championship game on the line. This was the moment in sports that I'd dreamt about my whole life. If I messed up, I'd regret it forever. If I got the job done, I'd remember it the rest of my life as a huge success.

The crowd was roaring, and it sounded like I was at an NFL game. I called the cadence and received the ball from the center. The noise from the crowd shut off instantly. All I could hear were echoes of the other players' voices as if I were in a sound bubble. Everything was in slow motion as I looked at Louis, the running back, as he plowed a hole for me up the middle by absolutely killing the middle linebacker, who had sacked me two plays before. But as soon as the hole opened, it closed. There was no time to think. Instincts took over, and I spun off the first defender. Before I knew it, I was on the other forty-five-yard line. More people were coming to get me. Another missed tackle, then another. Finally I had made it to the ten-yard line, and I was not going to settle for anything less than a touchdown. That was it. Game over. With thirty seconds left, there was no comeback for Lake O. The clock ran down and the Tualatin Valley Youth Football League champions were now the Oregon City Pioneers. It was one of the proudest moments in my life.

# Beach Trip

*Sam Harthun*

Sitting on the bus…waiting, waiting, waiting. We were on our way to Agate Beach, Oregon. We had headed to the beach as a school field trip in eighth grade. It took a total of about three hours to get there with lots of "educational" stops in between. I'm pretty sure it was Mr. Barrett's goal to cram every bit of info on sea life into our heads that he could.

Before we got to Agate Beach, we stopped to see the tide pools. We walked all over them, looking at all the sea life swimming and crawling or just sticking to rocks. The tide pools were beautiful, but I enjoyed Devil's Punch Bowl even more. Devil's Punch Bowl is a giant cave where waves wash in, making the most incredible view of the ocean. Luckily for us, the tide was out so we were able to enter the punch bowl. The water would wash up onto the rocks, foaming up and misting onto my face as I looked out at the ocean reaching back into the gray horizon.

While at the tide pools, our teacher, Mr. Kmetic, had warned us to watch our footing or we would fall in. Unfortunately for my friend Travis, the warning didn't help at all. He slipped on the seaweed that had been exposed from the tide being out, which happened to be, as Kmetic said, "very slippery." So Travis slipped and landed on some nasty green slime. The back of his pants got covered with it, and he was forced to walk around with green slime on his butt for the rest of the day. Lots of people fell that day, but luckily for me, I was not one of them.

When we finally got to Agate Beach, everybody was taking their shoes off and running and splashing in the water. Personally, I don't enjoy being cold and wet, so I stayed with one of my friends while most of our friends frolicked in the ice-cold water. Now, something they didn't consider is that, once you got your feet wet, there wasn't anything to get them dry. So, while they had fun on the beach at the time, they were miserable walking back up to the bus.

We were having just as much fun as any group of five-year-olds would while playing in the sand; the only difference was that we were a huge group of eighth-grade twelve-year-olds. We did everything that you would normally do at the beach, but we weren't allowed to go full-on swimming in the ocean, which happened to be fine with me, seeing as it was about fifty degrees on the Oregon Coast.

# Summer Picking—Summer Money

*Jacqueline Potter*

In the 1960s, the month of May meant school would soon be out. It also meant the berry farmers of Oregon would be coming to my school to entice students to pick berries during the summer. It was exciting to watch the reel-to-reel promotional movie of kids like myself picking berries and earning money! When I finished fourth grade, my time had come. I was old enough to join my older siblings before sunrise at the bus stop down the street for my first real job.

The school year ended and the picking season began. We made our lunches the night before picking day. They included peanut-butter-and-jelly sandwiches wrapped in waxed paper, and raisins and homemade molasses cookies. We froze cans of Shasta cream soda to add in the morning. I got out shorts and a t-shirt, long jeans, and a sweatshirt. Dressing in layers provided warmth in the cool mornings. Sturdy shoes were necessary too. No sandals were allowed.

The alarm clock rang in the darkness of morning. We got up, dressed, had breakfast quickly, then grabbed our lunches and walked down to the bus stop. There we were, a bunch of sleepy, cold kids, heading off to work. The bus stopped and we got on, sharing seats with friends and strangers, then off we went to the country. The "country" was the farmland east of Parkrose and the hills and land south of Gresham.

We arrived at the strawberry fields in the early dawn. Instructions were given on what was expected of us. There were stacks and stacks of large wooden berry crates, each with twelve pint-sized baskets inside. After being assigned a row to pick, we were shown how and what to pick. The berries needed to be red and firm. We needed to take off the stems as we picked. These were going to become jams and jellies. We were paid for each full crate we brought to the truck.

That first year I began to learn that hard work pays off. It was a privilege to have a job at such a young age. I felt useful and competent as I gained skills and a good work ethic, which have stuck with me throughout my life.

Strawberries, raspberries, blackcaps, marionberries, cucumbers, Blue Lake green beans, and hops—I picked them all, from that first summer until my junior year in high school. I looked forward to summertime out in the fields. The cool and quiet of the early morning, and the excitement of the noisy bus rides home each day with stained fingers and money in my pockets, are great memories.

Nowadays, I just pick huckleberries and black raspberries that grow wild in the Cascade Range. It is quiet and cool in the morning, hot in the afternoon, and my fingers get stained red with the sweet juice. It's like being a kid again.

# Epic Lightning Story

*Mikayla Friend*

At Lake Billy Chinook, in the summer of 2008, there was the oddest weather I have ever seen there. I have been camping there all my life—fourteen years, every summer. Lake Billy Chinook is a lake in the middle of the desert, but we camp far above the water at a campground called Crooked River Camp. We always go camping with our family friends. That year we had a camping site that was on the edge of the campground, so there was an enormous view of cacti, dry bushes, and desert behind us. Also, there was a power line behind us that ran to a transformer about fifty meters away.

Well, that year my friends and I decided to get spiritual, because we'd had mysterious things happen to us there before. While we were being goofy, I decided to do a "lightning dance," which called for lightning storms. Strangely enough, the lightning dance worked every time I did it. Even our parents asked me not to do the lightning dance anymore, because they were tired of the extreme weather.

The first time I did my "lightning dance," the biggest storm out of all of them came. When the lightning started, we had our friends and our family come into our trailer because we didn't want anyone getting struck by lightning. While we were in the trailer, the lightning storm worked its way over us. When it started to get really scary we turned on a movie for the kids, but later on the lightning started making the movie blink, so we had to turn it off and unplug the trailer in case a surge went through the power. When the thunder started to get louder, the little kids got very scared. It was funny though, because the parents kept telling them it was God moving furniture.

As the lightning started to come overhead, it struck out in the desert field behind us, and was followed by an earsplitting, echoing crack. A few seconds later was the best part: all of a sudden, there was the loudest crack of all. While we were looking outside, the lightning struck the pole only about twenty-five meters away from our trailer. It sizzled down the lines and blew out the transformer. The event kind of reminded me of the movie *War of the Worlds*.

# My Oregon

*Dallas Crone*

When I was little, I always thought my dream home would be far away from Oregon: somewhere in the Amazon, or in the Caribbean, on a deserted island where I would have some kind of monstrous mansion or a huge tree house in the jungle. I even wanted a submarine that was more like an underwater laboratory for a home. But when I started realizing that none of these fantasies would come true, I started noticing places that I, as a young boy, would never have thought of. Places of beauty, solitude, and tranquility stand out to me; I long for a place away from the hustle and bustle of life.

One place that has always caught my eye ever since I was a young, strapping boy is the Eagle Cap Mountains in northeastern Oregon. Just about every year my family and I go hunting over by the Snake River just beyond the mountains. The drive there is long and unforgiving, but I savor the last two hours—the flat, golden fields from La Grande to Joseph, and the rolling green hills, sometimes covered with a sheet of white. Every time it takes my breath away, and through this amazing scenery there are the Eagle Cap Mountains, standing tall and strong as the backdrop to tie the stunning view together. The long and majestic peaks cover most of northeastern Oregon.

Far into the Eagle Caps there is more beauty; for elk hunting, my family packs in on horseback into the Minam unit. It is a fifteen-mile ride out of the trailhead, past a little town in the mountains called Cove. The ride is rugged, long, and steep. We go to an area called Sturgill, which is located just off the Minam River. This sleek, swift current runs from the mountains down to the Snake on its long, winding voyage out to the ocean and it is usually stocked full of fish.

All this area is a dream come true to me. A place where I want to raise a family, grow old, and die. A place away from the city life and lights. No noise and nothing but clean air for my lungs to breathe. So the ideal spot for me to live would be in the Eagle Cap Mountains a couple miles out of Joseph. A secluded, peaceful log cabin tucked away in the long fingers of the mountains would be the home for me. I'd work from a computer and have my food and supplies air-dropped in. That would be the life; maybe I'd get married and share it with that special someone.

# Historic Oregon

This chapter contains historic tales of the important people, places, and events that made Oregon what it is today, including accounts of the intrepid pioneers who first traveled the Oregon Trail.

# My Oregon Story

## Governor Barbara Roberts

As Oregon prepares to celebrate our 150th anniversary of statehood, my head is filled with so many stories and memories that I would like to share. However, I have selected a personal story of a family search that seems perfect for this year of state celebration.

My family came to Oregon on the Oregon Trail in 1853. My great-great-grandparents, James and Almeda Boggs, both from Pennsylvania, left Iowa that spring with a wagon full of their worldly possessions; an ox team; three children ages ten, eight, and four; and—yet unknown to them—a baby on the way.

They arrived in October of 1853 to accept their donation land claim in Polk County. They had buried their eight-year-old daughter, who died of yellow fever on the trail. Almeda was seven months pregnant when she reached Oregon. The child she carried inside for every mile of that arduous journey was my great-grandmother Anna, born on January 1, 1854, the first member of my family to be born in Oregon.

Two years ago my younger son Mark and I traveled to southern Oregon on a mission of family-history gathering. We were searching for the head-stones of my Oregon Trail ancestors. We knew that, five years after reaching Oregon, they had traded their Polk County farm for another land grant farm in Douglas County. We believed they were buried in one of the many pioneer cemeteries in the Roseburg area. Yet the wear and ravages of 150 years made these sites difficult to identify.

Before his death, my dad had searched unsuccessfully for the markers in a number of cemeteries. My son and I decided we would search again.

We set aside three days for this adventure. We spent time in the county courthouse, Roseburg's city hall, and the county museum. With better information, we tromped through the first couple of burial grounds without success.

On our second day of searching, in the heat of August, we found our family at the Civil Bend Pioneer Cemetery in Winston. We found a double headstone, the final resting place of the pioneers who had made Oregon "home" for the next six generations of my family. We cleaned and polished the headstone, cleared the plot, and took out our cameras to record this moment, where past and present came together for our family. It was a very emotional "reunion" for me.

My great-great-grandparents lived to see Oregon become a state on February 14, 1859. Can you imagine what they would have felt knowing that one of their descendants would one day become not only an Oregon governor, but the first woman governor in our state's history?

I believe James and Almeda Boggs would have been almost as pleased and excited about my piece of history as I was to find their headstone and fill in that blank in our family's history.

I will always remain proud of my Oregon heritage.

# Bill Hansell
Umatilla County Commissioner
Oregon 150 Board of Directors

I was an eighth grader at Athena Grade School when the one hundredth birthday of Oregon rolled around. While my memories are fifty years old, I recall several things about the centennial. I kept a scrapbook; my grandmother embroidered shirts for all her grandchildren to wear, including my two brothers and me; and I had a centennial string tie.

Whenever I wore that embroidered shirt, I wore the centennial tie. Being a fourteen-year-old farm boy, I didn't own any ties except for that string tie. When I showed my 4-H pigs that year, I wore the centennial tie to all the livestock shows. Formal family photos in 1959 usually found that tie clipped to my collar.

Fast forward to the 150th birthday celebration, which finds that fourteen-year-old boy now a Umatilla County Commissioner and a member of the Oregon 150 Board of Directors. It has been a very rewarding experience for me to participate in planning the celebrations of Oregon's 150 years of statehood.

The one item of clothing I could still wear from fifty years previous, my string tie, was nowhere to be found. So when former Union County Commissioner Colleen McLoud offered to lend me her father's centennial string tie, I was elated. Because I was the only Oregon 150 Board member from northeast Oregon, I had the opportunity to speak about the sesquicentennial activities on numerous occasions, such as chamber meetings, service clubs, and other meetings. The string tie was worn, and I used it to illustrate and "tie" my remarks together. But I knew when the year ended I would have to return the borrowed tie to its owner.

Then the neatest thing happened. At the August meeting of the Oregon 150 Board, Board member Thomas Lauderdale brought his collection of around eight centennial string ties. He gave them to the Oregon 150 Chair, Oregon First Lady Mary Oberst, to hand them out, and I was fortunate to be given one. While it was a bit worn, I am thrilled to once again have a string tie from 1959. Sometime in the future I plan to pass it along to my thirteen-year-old grandson Luke. He can wear it when Oregon celebrates its bicentennial.

# That Remarkable Group of Women

*Katherine Keniston*

> "To me, as we grow, we don't have to necessarily be the first, or the biggest; we simply need to stay concerned for the poor and vulnerable and we need to meet the needs of people today. It is about how good we can be—in the service to others."
>
> —Sister Rita Ferschweiler, S.P.,
> Providence Health & Services in Oregon

While Oregonians were celebrating their new statehood in 1859, just across the Columbia River a remarkable group of five women were making history of their own. They had completed an arduous journey from Montreal, Quebec, two years earlier, stepping off a steamer at Fort Vancouver in the Washington Territory.

These pioneering Sisters of Providence, in their distinctive black habits, settled into a land where there were no hospitals, few schools, and scant charitable services for people suffering the misfortunes of frontier life. The sisters were led by a skilled carpenter and architect of great compassion and vision named Mother Joseph of the Sacred Heart. Equipped with simple tools, enormous gifts for creating and building, and a deep faith, Mother Joseph and her sister companions set to work teaching children and giving tender care to the poor and vulnerable.

The Sisters of Providence went on to build hospitals, schools, orphanages, homes for the elderly, and shelters for the mentally ill. In 1875 they established Oregon's first permanent hospital, St. Vincent Hospital, which began as a three-story wooden structure in northwest Portland.

> "Sometimes in dealing with...challenges, I think of that group of women.... I think of them facing great need with limited resources—and of their loving, giving hearts."
>
> —Russ Danielson, chief executive, Providence Health & Services in Oregon

121

Over the decades, the Sisters of Providence health care ministry has evolved into today's Providence Health & Services. People of Providence continue the sisters' work by living a mission of revealing "God's love for all, especially the poor and vulnerable, through our compassionate service." Providence serves communities in Oregon, Washington, Alaska, California, and Montana.

In Oregon, the not-for-profit Providence Health & Services operates seven hospitals: Providence St. Vincent Medical Center and Providence Portland Medical Center in Portland, Providence Milwaukie Hospital, Providence Hood River Memorial Hospital, Providence Newberg Medical Center, Providence Seaside Hospital, and Providence Medford Medical Center. Providence also includes physician clinics, health centers, home-care services, health plans, and care centers for medically fragile children and older adults. With some 16,000 employees, Providence is now Oregon's largest private employer.

Providence provided Oregonians with more than $165 million in community benefits during 2008, including more than $77 million in free care to patients in need. The work of serving the poor and vulnerable remains as real today as when Mother Joseph knelt to comfort an orphan child or to ease an elder's pain.

> "What is truly wonderful about working at Providence Medford Medical Center is that sense and feeling that the Sisters of Providence still walk our halls."
>
> —Elaine Ritchey, R.N.

# My Vision for this Good Land Called Oregon

## Jack McGowan
### Former Executive Director of SOLV

I am not a native-born Oregonian. However, my wife, Jan, is a fifth-generation Oregonian, and I'm proud to say that we added one more to the list with the birth of our son, Travis, over twenty-one years ago.

As I write this, I just shake my head as to my good fortune, having been born and raised in a tough, working class neighborhood in New York City. For it was New York and a certain Paul Simon that first gave me an inkling of what was to be my beloved home, Oregon.

In 1970, I was still a young man, entering my fourth year working on the floor of the New York Stock Exchange and living in a small, seven-story walk-up apartment in Greenwich Village on Manhattan's lower west side. After yet another stressful day of work, I'd climb those seven flights of stairs and seek refuge by entering into another chapter of Ken Kesey's *Sometimes A Great Notion*. Since I had never been west of New Jersey, this totally different land, laid forth in pages, intrigued me to no end.

My deep sense of lack of fulfillment as to who I was and where my life was headed increased, until finally I made the decision to leave the Exchange and New York and go somewhere west. This is where one chance encounter changed the course of my life for the much better.

Just prior to leaving New York for the last time, a friend (who now also calls Oregon his home) and I met the singer Paul Simon while we were all waiting for the light to change on a busy Manhattan city street corner. After discussing the war in Vietnam, the killings of Bobby Kennedy and Martin Luther King, Jr., and where our country was headed, the topic turned to our lives. I explained about my disillusionment with Wall Street and New York, and of my plans to head west the next week. It was Paul who said, "If you want a big city, try Seattle. If you want a town that thinks it's a city, try Portland." Needless to say, I chose the latter.

I arrived in my Oregon, without a family and not knowing a soul. This land has been good and gentle with me, for it gave me opportunities that I would not have found anywhere else. In Oregon, it is still the individual that can make things happen for good or ill. Over these thirty-nine years—by myself, then with friends, and then with family—I have traveled time and again Oregon's road less-traveled and witnessed her beauty until my eyes filled.

From watching the sunrise from the summit of Steens Mountain, to swimming in a little-known pool in the Malheur River, to watching the sun set from the most western point of the continental United States at Cape Blanco, this good land called Oregon gives us so much and asks so little in return.

With these gifts that were given to me, the most precious, next to my wife and our son, has been the honor of leading Governor Tom McCall's organization, SOLV*, for eighteen years. This, like no other experience, has given me some understanding of the fabric of Oregon.

Over those eighteen years, I traveled well over 200,000 miles throughout the state and met literally thousands of Oregonians as they helped each other in restoring degraded watersheds, cleaning beaches and illegal dump sites, removing invasive plant species and planting native ones in their place, and thousands of other projects.

The question, "Why do they do it?" has been answered with, "Because they simply care." What a simple, yet profound, statement.

My dream for our Oregon is that we, the people, do form a more perfect place by continuing to come together. That we do spend more time finding our commonalities and less time searching for our differences. That we pay less time listening to the naysayers and more time listening to one another, for the opposite of vision is division. That we become the volunteer capital of the United States, and hold on to that title as a statement of our values. And most importantly, that our legacy is held up as a tradition on Oregon's bicentennial.

*Editors' Note: SOLV was founded in 1969 as Stop Oregon Litter and Vandalism. Since then the organization has expanded their focus beyond that name and is now referred to simply as SOLV.

# Pine Street Coffee House 1895–1939

*Julie Crossley*

One of our Swiss ancestors came to Oregon in the late 1800s and ran the Pine Street Coffee House for years. His house, which is on the National Historic Register, is still standing on sw 1st Avenue. I had a vague memory of seeing a menu from the coffeehouse somewhere in the "pioneer chest" I inherited from my mother, so I dug through it and came up with a twenty-two-page publication written by my grandfather's uncle, Johan Gottlieb Haelen, in 1914, titled *Historical Sketch of the Pine Street Coffee House*. This delightful little book includes pictures and the early history of the city of Portland, as well as the story of the coffeehouse.

"Got," as he was known, was born in Lenk, Switzerland, and came to Portland via San Francisco in 1883. He and his brother opened the Knickerbocker coffeehouse on sw Washington at 4th Avenue. In 1895, they bought the Pine Street Coffee House for $700. It was located on nw Pine near 1st Avenue, on the pier that existed over the Willamette River before the seawall was built. People came from all over town for his German pancakes, waffles, or for ham and eggs; soon it became known as the "millionaire's club." The original structure was torn down in 1914, and the new location at 226 Pine Street thrived under Got's direction until its forty-fourth anniversary in 1939. The restaurant became a family affair. Four of his nephews worked there along with his brother-in-law, my great-grandfather.

# Questions for Grandma Carlson

*Anonymous*

Grandma, why did you hide
behind that rigid, self-sufficient mask,
rarely pulling that curtain aside
to let the soul show?

Were you scared, Grandma,
a too-young Finnish widow,
working your way from Michigan to Astoria,
creating clothes from newspaper patterns,
herding three little ones through train cars,
leaving your parents far behind?

Did you want to keep going
over the wild Pacific,
arrive in Japan or Taiwan,
make clothes from home-grown silk,
pile the children in rickshaws
and learn to use chopsticks?

Or did you feel at home right away
in Oregon, the state that gave you another husband,
a tight-lipped Swede whom you once chased
with a frying pan, and who sired
your next four children?

Did you take to your bed, Grandma,
when your eldest son fell from a paddle-wheeler
into the Willamette and drowned,
like your daughter, our mother did,
when her eldest succumbed to polio?

Did you ever guess, Grandma, that your descendants
would cross the oceans many times,
fight in wars, ride in pedicabs and kamikaze taxis,
wade through typhoon debris, learn to eat sushi,
live in Africa where your great-grandson teased
six foot cobras, hunt ancestors in Finland,
explore Europe, yet always rush
eagerly back to Oregon where they raised
more little ones than you could have imagined
when you willed your way west
and became our own pioneer, Grandma?

# The Sitka Spruce at Klootchy Creek

*The Oregon Travel Information Council*

T he Sitka Spruce at Klootchy Creek (*Picea sitchensis*) was the first tree to be designated an official Oregon Heritage Tree, and was once the biggest tree in Oregon as well as the National Co-champion Sitka Spruce. It germinated from a seed on the forest floor around the time of the signing of the Magna Carta in 1215, and grew to its mature height at about the time Christopher Columbus sailed to the new world. A legacy of the primeval coastal old-growth rain forests of the Pacific Northwest, the Sitka Spruce was also remarkable for having been bypassed for logging when spruce was in high demand for building military aircraft; it was considered to have too many limbs to meet the standards of the national aircraft board.

Sadly, this once-magnificent tree suffered severe damage on December 2, 2007, when hurricane-force winds snapped the tree about eighty feet above ground along an old lightning scar. The top portion shattered as it hit the ground. Aware of the tree's significance, Clatsop County officials decided to let the trunk stand and leave the pieces on the ground to rot and provide nutrients for future Sitka giants. New interpretive signs will be developed to tell the history of the Klootchy Creek Giant and about the natural life cycle of trees in the forest.

The Sitka Spruce is located on U.S. Highway 26 in Klootchy Creek County Park, two and a half miles east of the junction with U.S. Highway 101. It is 216 feet tall with a circumference of fifty-six feet and a crown spread of ninety-three feet; it is estimated to be more than 750 years old.

# Timberline Lodge: A Place in History

## Jon Tullis
DIRECTOR OF PUBLIC AFFAIRS, TIMBERLINE LODGE

Timberline Lodge is one of Oregon's sixteen National Historic Landmarks. Ordinarily, properties need to be at least fifty years old to be considered for this important designation; it is felt that time must pass in order for a landmark to be considered significant. That makes sense when you consider the term "historic" and remember that these landmarks are joining the vanguard of such hallowed places in American history as Monticello, Mount Vernon, the Alamo, and the White House. But in 1977, just forty years after the lodge was built as the Northwest's crowning jewel in Franklin Roosevelt's New Deal Works Progress Administration (WPA), the significance of that time period and all that Timberline represents was apparent enough for this designation to be bestowed upon the lodge. Timberline Lodge is certainly the most magnificent example of an inspired style of regional architecture now known as "Cascadian," but that alone does not warrant historic landmark status. Fundamentally, Timberline was chosen as a National Historic Landmark for its significance in representing a pivotal period of time in our nation's history, a time when a new course for government was set with the bold notion that government has the strength and the power, when working with its citizenry, to provide solutions to our biggest problems. This notion was made manifest in spectacular public works such as Timberline Lodge. Timberline was born with this sense of determination, resourcefulness, and an egalitarian ideal. Timberline Lodge was truly built "by the people, for the people."

Today, we are recognizing the seventy-fifth anniversary of the New Deal, and many people are yearning for a modern-day WPA of sorts. In my position as Director of Public Affairs for Timberline Lodge, I find it interesting to hear from them. Timberline stands today not just as an icon of Oregon, but as a symbol of New Deal political thought. Specifically, it represents the objectives of the New Deal's Federal Art Project, which funded the building of Timberline. During the wpa's broad-reaching dedication to public works, decorative arts and crafts were valued just as much as practical infrastructure. Craftsmanship provided a source of pride and a focus on old-world quality, as well as an opportunity to learn a trade. Painting and graphic arts in particular provided inspiration and an expression of the New Deal movement, and, in a not-so-subtle way, it often promoted the New Deal itself. This is showcased at Timberline with wpa murals such as Howard Sewell's "Metal" and "Wood," which depict craftsmanship in a strict and purposed fashion. Such works, particularly wpa poster art, served almost as democratic propaganda and spoke of determination, progress, hard work, and the power of the people.

America at the time was in the throes of the Great Depression, and these so-called "make work" projects became a pivotal part of Roosevelt's New Deal plans to address an idled economy, high unemployment, and the prevalent hunger, despair, and sense of aimlessness that resulted. At the time, the power of the American industrialists and the wealthy elite was tantamount to a ruling class. The country was suffering the worst economic period in its history, social unrest was on the rise, and the nation's political system was being brought into question. There was talk among some that the American "experiment" had simply failed.

Franklin Delano Roosevelt wouldn't accept that. He closed his acceptance speech at the Democratic National Convention in Chicago by saying, "I pledge you, I pledge myself, to a new deal for the American people." That "new deal" became what we now know as the historic New Deal, a sweeping set of social programs and policies that set the agenda for the era. The Democratic nominee began to craft what he thought the role of the government should be in society and in the economy.

His biggest objective was to bring jobs to the people and pull economic power under control, for the good of all the people. It was a bold and populist thought. He was literally redefining freedom, progress, and government. The people rallied behind him and his plans for both a bigger government and a stronger middle class, and he went on to win the presidency in 1932. In his first term he brought the banks under federal regulation, and he brought us social security, a minimum wage, subsidized housing, and unemployment insurance—things that he felt the free market couldn't completely create, much less guarantee.

His administration then turned their focus to job creation. Federal public works projects included the construction of roads, bridges, schools, post offices, and perhaps most significantly, dams to generate electricity for rural areas. Here in the West, public lands and the roles of federal land managers were expanded. The Forest Service rolled out land allocations that were until then stored quietly in planning documents upon shelves. The Civilian Conservation Corps (CCC) and the WPA built trails, campgrounds, picnic areas, water systems, and ranger stations. And here on Mount Hood, they built a spectacular ski lodge, which Roosevelt dedicated on September 28, 1937, "as a monument to the skill and faithful performance of workers on the rolls of the Works Progress Administration." At the time, Roosevelt was on a two-week tour of Oregon and visited many of his New Deal accomplishments. In his dedication of the near-complete Bonneville Dam, he underscored his public works philosophy: "Instead of spending, as some nations do, half of their national income in piling up armaments…we in America are wiser in using our wealth on projects like this, which will give us more wealth, better living, and greater happiness for our children."

Working at Timberline, I have always thought that I understood the importance of the social history to which the lodge belongs, but it seemed like just that—distant history. Lately, however, I wonder if we now will perhaps come to know firsthand the significance of these challenges, and how they could inspire and motivate people to create something like Timberline Lodge. Today, our nation once again faces similar dismay, and there is talk of a new New Deal, one for the twenty-first century. Perhaps, as some have proposed, this could be a green New Deal that invests primarily in public works projects that utilize and promote new energy technologies. Attention to infrastructure throughout the country is critically overdue. Certainly, and perhaps ironically, the aging projects and buildings built during the WPA are now facing natural deterioration themselves. Our own Governor Ted Kulongoski has recently presented a clever initiative for the Obama administration to consider; his so-called "Campus Project" would focus public works efforts on the backlog of deferred maintenance at the nation's many state universities. The Obama administration is listening.

Certainly, a lot has changed in the last seventy-five years, and I listen with amazement as "futurists" discuss what change society is likely to bring us in the years to come, but right now, in December of 2008, I'm glancing backward. There seem to be striking parallels between today and the domestic affairs of America in the 1930s. Once again, wealth has become gradually polarized in our social strata, the gap between the haves and the have-nots has widened, there is very real economic trouble, the stock market is faltering, unemployment is on the rise, and the American people are increasingly becoming disenfranchised and desperate. These things are once again in the news, and on the political front there is much talk about "change" and "hope" and "a new beginning." It strikes me that the message and style of Barack Obama's presidency are very similar to Roosevelt's. He is engaging the people in dialogue, sharing concerns, speaking frankly, framing a common cause, and challenging us to a shared sacrifice. This is just what Roosevelt did in his famous "fireside chats." Even the Obama "Hope" posters recall the WPA posters that echoed the rallying cries of the day.

The other day, my phone rang here at Timberline Lodge. On the other end was a wonderful woman in her eighties. She said that she had been to Timberline the week before, and just couldn't shake the memories and the sense of hope that the place had given her. It reminded her of the Great Depression through which she had lived, and of the hope and purpose that the New Deal public works projects provided. She remembered it all, and said, "If this country falls into another economic depression, it is going to take projects like Timberline to pull us out of it." She said she hoped that "your generation," as she kept referring to it, "was up to it and would rise to the challenge." She said, "You have such a powerful symbol up there! I hope people remember their history." She went on to describe herself as a "dyed-in-the-wool Republican," but then shared with me that she was going to vote for Barack Obama. "Things need to change," she said.

As I ponder our conversation, I am reminded that our future lies in preserving our history. While it is a stretch to propose that Timberline Lodge is once again at the crossroads of history, it feels like history itself is shouting up the street to us, hoping that we will listen and consider where we are. Such a phone call also renews one of our most solemn purposes here as operators of Timberline Lodge, that of historic preservation through use. And it doesn't stop with us. At Oregon's 150th anniversary of statehood, all Oregonians can be proud of this great place for its accomplishments, its history, and its symbolic value.

# Columbus Day, 1962

*Minnette Meador*

It was Friday, October 12, 1962. My parents worked to support the five of us, so my sister saw me off to school. She had to leave early that morning, so just a thin sweater for me; who needed a coat on such a fine, sunny day?

I sat behind giant mullioned windows in the second-grade classroom, watching half-naked trees through the glass. Nothing was moving. The sky looked odd; black frozen clouds loomed above the playground, swings hung black and silver against the cyclone fence, steel merry-go-rounds were dusted with leaves. The teacher droned on about some man traveling on a voyage with three tiny ships who found himself lost on his way to "The New World."

Something stirred. A rain drop, then ten, then fifty broke the fragile leaves scattered on the ground, pounded the metal rides and tin roof. The drumming was so loud, we couldn't hear the teacher's voice anymore. She glanced through the panes of glass and frowned. The assembly bell's ding-ding-ding merged with the hiss of the clamoring rain.

They sent us home.

No yellow bus for me—too close to home. I walked out into the rain, the cold drops chilling my flushed cheeks.

The rain started as an adventure. I gathered my legs together, ran the first block—*no school!*—and splashed into deep puddles, my patent-leather shoes repelling the water, looking slick as oil. My clothes were drenched in seconds, the sweater clinging to me like blistered skin. The pouring sky went from pleasant patters to sheets of pain, the hail stinging my little face and hands. I hugged a tree until it passed.

I was scared now.

The wind blew so hard I couldn't see more than a beach ball's throw in front of me. The motion of cars whipping through the haze a block away was the only other movement. I was cold, hurt, crying. The wind howled like a pack of hungry dogs, and I ran.

I don't know how I made it home that day. My mother was there when I burst through the door in hysterics, the winds behind me smacking it against the wall. She tamed the door, bundled me up in a warm towel, and nestled my shivering body into a hot bath. Nothing since has ever felt so glorious.

The storm grew into a cyclone. I remember watching two plate-glass windows bow under the pressure of the gusts. We clung to one another in front of the fire, the power long gone. My father was with the National Guard, lost somewhere in the city battling the storm—a white knight, his sword drawn, slaying the monster. He was actually hauling sandbags to keep the rising river from destroying downtown.

We spent the night in the basement. The only losses were small windows, my mother's nerves, and my confidence. Everything else escaped unscathed.

I think of it now, many years later, and still shiver a little. Pelting rain. Cyclone winds. Columbus Day.

# Early Life on the Farm

*Hugh Mount*

Hanson and Lavina Stevens made their way west on the Oregon Trail and arrived in Oregon City on June 15th, 1853. Hanson and Lavina made a land claim and were granted a 320-acre plot of land on the west bank of the Pudding River. Married settlers arriving before December 1, 1850, were awarded 640 acres, half of which would be taken in the wife's name in her own right.

There remain only a few reminiscences of their early life on the farm. In one story, Lavina was reportedly alone in the cabin when she noticed some Native Americans at the window. They indicated that they were hungry, so she opened the door and gave them some of her freshly baked bread. The next morning Hanson opened the door to find a newly killed deer on their doorstep in payment for the bread. They had heard no sound during the night.

Hanson and Lavina are buried side by side at the Bethany Cemetery near Silverton.

# The Reverend Robert Robe

*Marcia Allen*

Born October 10, 1822 in Ohio, Robert Robe was the youngest in a family of three sons and five daughters. They were raised by a father who was an active church worker and a strict disciplinarian as well as a large landowner. He attended Western Theological Seminary in Allegheny, Pennsylvania, and upon graduation was armed with his Bible and a metal tube containing his graduation diploma written in Latin on sheepskin—a true Minister of the gospel.

He planned to marry his intended wife and leave for Oregon on the wagon trains that were forming in St. Jo to serve as a missionary in the West, perhaps with Marcus Whitman. His wife-to-be, however, refused to think about such a life. So, without any provisions except his Bible, Reverend Robe volunteered to help drive and guard stock on the wagon train in exchange for his food. Without a horse to ride, except for one borrowed when guarding the cattle and horses during the night, he walked all the way to Oregon. He had a strong tenor voice and led singing around the camp-fires at night with the aid of a tuning fork. He kept a daily diary on the Trail, which the Robe family still has in their possession.

Upon arriving in Oregon, he signed the registry at the Umatilla Agency on August 25, 1851. When he left the wagon train, he contacted the other two Presbyterian ministers in the Oregon Territory and met with them to organize and establish the first Presbytery of Oregon. The boundary of the Oregon Presbytery was the Rogue River valley on the south, the foothills of the Rocky Mountains on the east, and the upper waters of the Columbia River and Puget Sound on the north. A single church of four members existed at the time, near Astoria. Reverend Robe sailed by steamer from Portland to San Francisco to register the necessary church papers. Upon his return to Oregon, he taught a pioneer school for three months "in the wilderness" near Brownsville. He then moved to Eugene, where he claimed a homestead, built a dwelling, and married Eliza Walker, who had recently come from Georgia.

He organized the First Presbyterian Church in Eugene under an oak tree on the southwest corner of 10th and Willamette in 1855, and served as its pastor for the next ten years. At the same time, he served as an itinerant minister throughout the Presbytery and was often gone for long periods to assist the new immigrants by preaching and performing weddings and burials as necessary. He was also the first superintendent of Lane County Schools.

After ten years, in 1865, Reverend Robe moved to Brownsville, where a church was already established, and served there for thirty years until his retirement in 1895. During this time he organized the church in Crawfordsville. To this day, a large memorial window in the front of the Brownsville Presbyterian Church reads "Rev. Robert Robe" on red glass. It has lasted through two fires.

He was the father of eleven children, seven of whom died in the dreaded diphtheria epidemics, for which there was no known medicine. He raised three sons and a daughter (who was my grandmother), and died in 1909 at the age of eighty-six.

# Celilo

## *Rebecca Phinney*

S itting in my bedroom, the lights dimmed, no one else in the house, I hear it. The roar of the falls fills my ears. I see the tumultuous river foaming over basalt stair-steps. I see the dip-netters of Celilo, bracing themselves on the slippery wooden scaffold, holding their poles over the froth, the fifty-pound-plus fish falling into their nets as the salmon fight their way back toward their spawning grounds. The sights, the sounds, the smells, engulf me and, overcome by the majesty of what I see and feel, I rise, open my eyes, and shrivel with disappointment. I have not seen the falls. I will never see the falls.

I am still in my room, swallowing my rage at the helplessness I feel when I look upon this horrible travesty wrought upon nature. I feel sick with grief at the connection I have and the responsibility I feel for the drowning of a culture. I keep my guilt and anger tucked away, afraid of being seen hypocritical if I let it show. I was born too late to stop the event I loathe with my entirety now. Though I long to see the falls, I see nothing but cold, grey cement and the lake behind it.

I cannot remember, but I know. Fifty years ago, the dam went up. The spill gates closed. The people of Celilo Village stood weeping on the banks as the water rose, silencing the thunder of the falls. Their ancient village, along with homes, graves, and memories, was buried beneath the mockingly placid pool of water. They were left with nowhere to live, squished between railroad and rock, in the deserted barracks of the people who built the concrete beast that destroyed their old homes.

Their children were taken and forced to attend boarding schools where they were not allowed to practice their religion or speak in their native tongues. They were force-fed English and Christianity, and verbally and physically abused. The village of Celilo wilted. With barely enough salmon to support Celilo, the tribes that had once come from as far away as the

Great Plains to fish and trade stayed away. The once-booming economic hub became a sad recollection of grander days, the ghost of something once remarkable.

The native word for Celilo Falls, *Wyam*, means "sound of water upon rocks," or "echo of falling water." To me, Celilo means sorrow; irrational guilt; irrevocable destruction of a landmark, a people, a culture, a history. It is a billboard of the white man's money lust; profit from progress for progress' sake. I close my eyes and submerge myself in the magnificence of the falls, which I can only ever see and hear inside my head.

# The Last Person to Hang from the Gallows in Salem

## Debbe von Blumenstein

My father, Lynn von Blumenstein, was a treasure hunter throughout Oregon, and even found a mammoth tooth in Champoeg Park, but his adventurous spirit came from his mother, my grandmother, Mickey Endicott Blumenstein. She was a spotter during the war, reporting to the government when airplanes were seen overhead in the area. Through that connection she was able to make other connections, so that, when Salem decided to tear down the gallows, she was able to make a special request. As a writer, she wanted to experience life and try to walk in other people's shoes, so she asked permission to walk the thirteen steps to the gallows, in order to try to experience what the condemned might feel. Her request was granted, but as she reached the platform, she lost her balance because of the heels she was wearing, and her feet went out from under her. To stop herself from falling, she reached up and grabbed the rope of the noose. The trap door sprung open, and there she hung—so my grandmother was the last person to ever hang from the gallows in Salem.

# Fort Clatsop

*Sandra Ellston*

So thick the canopy of spruce and pine
that shadows pool in shades of hunter-teal,
lending to duff-piled paths a darkened mood
of solitude—or claustrophobia.
What change they found from bison-spotted plains
and alpine ridges pleated to the skies;
water had been their element through miles
of rough travail. These forests dripped like sieves.
The fort they meant as hopeful log-made ark,
refuge from endless stride and portage long,
a place to take stock of maps and journal notes—
tinder-dry bunks with giant stumps for desks,
enclosure self-contained, exclusive home,
quarter to heroes.

After such expanse
of destiny manifest to fertile minds,
this tiny fort, potential outpost safe,
seems toy-like now. We grin through window sash,
peer into larder-room hung with dried pelts,
pretend to stir the coals of cooking fire,
and write in jest at Lewis's secret'ry.
There is a kind of human needs to rove,
the character composed of getting there,
made real to us in Appleseeds and Boones,
in Bumppos, and now Lewis, York, and Clark.

Can we feel anticlimax of that year,
Eighteen-oh-five, eighteen-oh-six, so wet
they doubted this was truly promised land?
The roof boards leaked; humidity was high;
they needed river near for drinking source,
yet moisture drowned their spirit month by month.
The air was redolent with smell of damp;
ironically, they sought out the great sea
as well to render salt and minerals.
Their moist minds dwelt on traveling back home.
They thought of Jefferson and his grand thanks.
They sketched and named and reminisced in ink.
They nestled in and hunkered down and slept.

Whoever knows the ends our journeys make?
They sought the last perimeter of earth
yet found it more than mind could have conceived.
In that explorers' journey farthest west
young Meriwether lost his will to live,
and those of us now heirs unto this place
think not too much of natives, conquerors,
deem this our land, our well-earned paradise.

# Journey to Damascus

## Sue Fagalde Lick

I sit cross-legged on a dry patch of grass in the Damascus Pioneer Cemetery and introduce myself to Refucia Maria Alviso and Jean Fagalde, my great-great-grandparents on my dad's father's side. My husband, Fred, and I, California refugees, only live three hours away in South Beach, but it took quite a journey to find this spot.

It began with the internet discovery that Refucia, Jean, and their son John were buried there. When my father and my brother Mike came to visit, we drove to this tiny town southeast of Portland to look for our roots. The weather was clear and pleasantly warm. We wandered all over the cemetery, reading good old names like Daisy and Amos and Eulalia, but no Fagaldes. Whatever stone or wooden markers might have been placed on the Fagalde graves had disintegrated over time. After all, Jean died in 1883 (or maybe 1886). But if they were on the list, someone would know where they were buried.

We stopped at Damascus City Hall. A young woman came out of the cubicles to greet us. We told her that our relatives had settled here in the 1800s, and that we knew they were buried in the cemetery, but we couldn't find any stones. Who might know about this? She directed us to City Councilwoman Barbara Ledbury, who was thrilled to hear from me. She had paid for an expensive radar search to locate her family and had found the Fagalde graves next door.

Barbara couldn't meet with us that day, but we had one more stop to make. According to the 1870 census, the Fagaldes lived at the junction of Deep Creek and the Clackamas River. We headed down a country road past barns and fields of tall grass, passed a school, and came to the creek. As the creek grew into the wide Clackamas River, we imagined Jean and Refucia and their thirteen children farming this land.

Jean was born in France; Refucia came from Baja California. His family had a chocolate factory in Cambo-les-Bains. Her father or grandfather was part of the De Anza Expedition that founded San Francisco. How did they get together?

Eight of their thirteen children were born in California, the others in Oregon. One of those Oregon-born Fagaldes was my great-grandfather, Joseph Burt Fagalde, who married Louisa Gilroy and settled in San Jose, California, my hometown. But perhaps we're Oregonians after all.

Months later, Fred and I meet Barbara at the cemetery. She shows us exactly where the graves are. The Fagalde plots are still unmarked, but I sit in the middle of them and start talking. I explain that I am Susan, daughter of Clarence, Jr., who was the son of Clarence Sr., whose father was their son Joseph. I tell them I am a writer and a musician, and that I hope they would be proud of this middle-aged, blue-jeaned woman sitting atop their grave. Someday we will give them the markers they deserve. Meanwhile, we have a lot of catching up to do.

# Volcano Weather: May 19, 1980

*Kathy Haynie*

The day was silent, and I was alone. The children were indoors, asleep for their naps. We didn't have a television, so I was going by what I'd heard from my gossipy next-door neighbor. Call me young, call me naive—all I wanted was to do the right thing.

I really thought the sky would rain ash. Mount St. Helens, about one hundred miles to the north of us, had erupted the day before. The next day, Monday, May 19, 1980, I didn't know whether to feel desperate or foolish as I spread the sheets of newspaper over the seedlings in our garden.

This was my first spring in the Northwest, and I was doing anything I could to encourage the growth of "webs" between my toes. During my first six months as an Oregonian, I had learned to take the weather seriously. Portland was so much colder than I had imagined. We were heating our eighty-year-old farmhouse with just a woodstove. Temperature mattered; I wanted my children to be warm and healthy. On the other hand, I had also learned *not* to take the weather too seriously. This wasn't Alaska, after all, and it was only a little drizzle, so what was the big deal? The children weren't going to melt from a little rain.

In the spring of 1980, I was so anxious to plant a garden that my first round of seeds rotted in the wet ground. By the end of April, the ground was drying out enough for real planting; by the middle of May, brave little pepper, tomato, lettuce, and potato plants were rearing their green heads. After the long, gray winter, I was anxious for greenery and fresh vegetables.

But now Mount St. Helens had finally erupted. We had been waiting for it for weeks, and the day before, on the way home from church, we had seen her column of ash tower into the afternoon sky. The Monday morning paper was full of photos of Yakima, Washington, dark at mid-afternoon, with several inches of ash accumulation raining down. Word was that the winds would probably shift, bringing the Portland area a

146

couple of inches of ash; we all went out and bought dust masks and worried what the ash would do to our vehicles' air filters.

It was strange, waiting for the ash to fall from that still, gray sky. On Tuesday I went back out to the garden, sheepishly, hoping the neighbors wouldn't notice as I gathered up the newspapers, clean of all that ash that never fell.

If the sky had fallen on Oregon City that day, it would have been terrible. People with lung disease would have taken ill, cars would have broken down, gardens might have been smothered in all that ash. We would have had to help each other; we might have struggled to survive.

If.

But that's a story that didn't happen.

# Oregon's Moon Tree

## The Oregon Travel Information Council

The Moon Tree (*Pseudotsuga menziesii*) is a Rocky Mountain Douglas fir that was raised from a seed carried to the moon by Apollo 14 astronaut Stuart Roosa in 1971.

Although Roosa had grown up in Oklahoma, he was no stranger to Oregon. While in college, he worked summers here as a smoke jumper and as a surveyor. Roosa trained to be an astronaut in eastern Oregon and later returned to hunt elk and duck. After his historic flight, Roosa expressed his strong ties with Oregon by choosing to have his official homecoming parade in Coos Bay.

Stuart Roosa took more than four hundred seeds to orbit the moon with him in his personal property kit. Most of the seeds successfully germinated and, after some nursery time, were distributed to many states and several foreign countries to celebrate America's bicentennial.

This Moon Tree was planted by Governor Bob Straub on Arbor Day, April 30, 1976. The tree's original seed came from Corvallis. The Moon Tree is located near Court Street in downtown Salem, in Willson Park to the west of the Capitol building. It is sixty-three feet tall with a nineteen-inch circumference; it is thirty-one years old.

# At the 1855 Treaty Negotiations the Tribal Chiefs Stated: "It is for the Children that We Do This..."

## Antone Minthorn

MEMBER, CONFEDERATED TRIBES OF THE
UMATILLA INDIAN RESERVATION

My name is Antone Minthorn, and I am a member of the Confederated Tribes of the Umatilla Indian Reservation. I am of the Cayuse/Nez Perce and Umatilla nation. I was born on the Umatilla Indian Reservation on January 27, 1935. Actually, I was born at St. Anthony's Hospital in Pendleton, Oregon, which was once a part of the original Umatilla Indian Reservation.

I was raised by my grandfather and grandmother. My grandfather was a Cayuse, and my grandmother was Nez Perce. My grandmother gave me an Indian name, which translates to "Big Dawn." I learned the Nez Perce dialect by talking with my grandmother. There are almost no fluent speakers of the Nez Perce dialect on the Umatilla Indian Reservation, but we do have a tribal languages program that works with Nez Perce, Umatilla, and Walla Walla dialects. One day I hope to hear these languages spoken again in our native community. I began my education at St. Andrew's Catholic Mission School on the reservation in 1941 and learned how to use the English language. The first word I remember the Sisters teaching me was, "TH-ink (think)."

In 1955, I was a college student at Gonzaga University in Spokane, Washington. When I came home for the summer break I stopped in Walla Walla, Washington, where there was a public event commemorating the Treaty of 1855. The city of Walla Walla was the site of the treaty council grounds. It was the place where the decision had been made, in treaty negotiations with the federal government, that the Cayuse, Umatilla, and

Walla Walla tribes would agree to the Umatilla Indian Reservation, located in Oregon Territory, as their homeland. There were also two other Indian Reservations established: Yakama and Nez Perce, both in Washington Territory.

What I found out much later, as I read the minutes of the 1855 Treaty negotiations, was that our tribal negotiators always held a great concern for a place where the children could live; that is, there had to be a place for those yet to come. When I finally realized what our leaders meant, I was deeply moved, because it was us today they were talking about. Our ancestors understood the value of land and children and stood by those principles, and that is the reason I have a home and place to live. However, I too am obligated to make good decisions for the safety of those children yet to come.

Our 1855 Treaty with the U.S. Government was ratified by Congress in 1859, the same year the state of Oregon was established. The Cayuse, Umatilla, and Walla Walla tribes moved onto the newly created 512,000-acre Umatilla Indian Reservation around that time. A treaty signed with the U.S. Government is the law of the land.

It was when the treaty was signed that the tribes lost much of their sovereignty, or the right to manage their own affairs. In the treaty document, there were stipulations that the Confederated Tribes consent to a dependence upon the federal government. In this respect, the office of the federal Indian agent, that is, the Bureau of Indian Affairs (BIA), became the chief manager of tribal affairs.

At the time of the treaty signing, the tribes were prosperous and owned millions of acres of land and thousands of head of stock in cattle and horses. As the federal policy changed, the tribes lost almost all of their land due to hostile federal legislation called the Allotment Act. This legislation parceled up the Indian reservation land into lots for each tribal member. The result was a reduced Umatilla Indian Reservation of 172,000 acres, and it generally remains the same today.

The tribes' dependent relationship with the Bureau of Indian Affairs (i.e., the federal government) introduced the possibility of losing the entire Umatilla Indian Reservation. In fact, some western Oregon tribes did lose their original Indian reservations, but have since been restored to federal recognition status and are now self-governing. The federal law that destroyed the land base of the western Oregon tribes was called Termination and was initiated in 1953.

From the time of early contact with the white people, before the treaty signings, the relationship has always been guarded. Our tribes, the Cayuse, Umatilla, and Walla Walla, fought the military and political battles to survive. We have triumphed, but there is still so much work to be done to rebuild our tribal national government.

The Confederated Tribes of the Umatilla Indian Reservation (Cayuse, Umatilla, and Walla Walla) has reestablished its sovereignty and works on a government-to-government basis with federal and state agencies. By working cooperatively, we are able to build a strong tribal government, providing essential services and a strong economy to help people make a living. The Umatilla tribes now employ over 1,300 people. We could never accomplish such goals by dependence on the federal government. For Native American tribal communities in Oregon, the best way to preserve culture is to have a strong economy and the right to make our own decisions.

The state of Oregon has been a national leader in promoting good government-to-government relationships with Oregon tribes. However, our relationship with Oregon, prior to the 1980s, was very hostile. Therefore, our goal for the next fifty years is not to go back to those times of hostility, but to work to strengthen our government-to-government relationships and our communities so that, together, we can help our people live good lives and learn to respect one another's cultures.

Finally, it is our hope and vision that the 1855 Treaty of the Cayuse, Umatilla, and Walla Walla tribes be honored by the federal and state governments and their people, because it is the right and just thing to do, but also because it is important to understand the powerful inherent authority tribes possess to help Oregon leaders achieve better government and create a stronger economy to help the people and the children. Furthermore, I believe the Umatilla Tribes Nation will again prosper and be a powerful economic and political force in the State of Oregon.

These are my thoughts for Oregon's sesquicentennial.

# School Kids and State Lands

*Julie Lindstrom Curtis*

COMMUNICATION MANAGER, OREGON DEPARTMENT OF STATE LANDS

Oregon—the "Eden at the End of the Oregon Trail"—was land-rich and cash-poor at its statehood in 1859. As scores of families came west to settle and prosper, the new state had few resources with which to educate their children.

Realizing this challenge, the federal government granted Oregon two square miles out of each township (a thirty-six-square-mile parcel), or approximately 3.4 million acres of land, to finance public schools.

Oregon's Constitution established the State Land Board—which is still composed of the Governor, Secretary of State, and State Treasurer—to oversee the new state's school lands.

Many of these lands were quickly sold, as public officials felt private ownership would yield more for schools through property taxes and other economic benefits. Although school lands were sold for between $1.25 and $2.50 an acre, safeguards were put in place to limit the number of acres an individual could purchase.

Revenue from land sales seeded the Common School Fund, a trust fund for schools that now has a market value of just under $1 billion. The State Land Board distributes earnings from the fund twice a year to Oregon's 198 K–12 public school districts. The two distributions in 2008 totaled $55.4 million.

But here's the interesting part—and a dark piece of Oregon history most citizens don't know and may be surprised to learn: In the early 1900s, thirty-three people were sent to prison as a result of the Oregon Land Fraud Scandal, a scheme aided by public officials whereby land speculators—or their "front men"—obtained large tracts of land illegally, offering kickbacks to those who facilitated the land grab.

*Looters of the Public Domain*, written by land-fraud kingpin Stephen A. Douglas Puter from his jail cell in 1908, exposed the details of the conspiracy that divested Oregon of nearly three-fourths of its school land, including thousands of acres of prime timberland worth many millions of dollars today.

Although the state will never get those lands back, the Department of State Lands (DSL) and the Land Board are committed to managing our current real estate portfolio to significantly increase the Common School Fund over time. Through selling nonproductive, isolated parcels and reinvesting in higher-earning lands, the department is making long-term investments for Oregon's schoolchildren.

DSL also is working to square up a 150-year-old debt of an additional 5,200 acres that the federal government still owes the state. Approximately 3,000 acres have been transferred to the state, and another 2,200 acres are in process. Most of the acreage is in the central Oregon area.

After 150 years of statehood, Oregon deserves well-managed school lands, and the Department of State Lands is delivering on that promise.

# Mill Town

Gilchrist, in Central Oregon, was the last company-owned town in Oregon. Gilchrist Timber Company founded the town when it moved its family-owned operation from Mississippi in 1938. My family moved to Gilchrist in 1966 when my father acquired a stake in the local grocery store. The timber company owned all the houses and most of the other buildings in town, including a movie theater, a restaurant, a two-lane bowling alley, and a post office, while my father and his partners owned the grocery business.

When my family arrived from suburban Portland, the streets in Gilchrist were still dirt, all the buildings were covered in the same brown paint, and many of the Mississippi transplants still survived. It was not uncommon to hear a customer drawling their order to the meat cutter. My dad carried on the practice of allowing local customers to charge their groceries until payday, and the timber company fronted the store currency to cash millworkers' paychecks, a service to employees since the nearest bank was forty-five miles away in Bend.

Gilchrist Timber Company owned over 100,000 acres of timberland around the town—a perfect place to make forts and ride bikes when young, and do other things when a little older. The forest was also the source of the town's livelihood. That changed when the Gilchrist family sold the mill and forestland in 1991 but retained the town, which was then subdivided and sold off house by house.

# My Mother, Alice Clark Tomlin, and How She Became a Teacher

## Carla Tomlin Mundt

My mother, Alice Clark Tomlin, was a second-generation Oregonian born in 1901 in Ukiah, Oregon. Her first full term of school was at age ten; in 1919 she was in eighth grade. By this time her mother had had fifteen births. In 1923, at age twenty-two, she was the only graduate from the Helix, Oregon, high school. The townspeople and farmers turned out to see her graduate.

In her earlier years her folks had told her that she was to be a teacher, and her papa used to make her brothers sit and play school with her. Tragedy then struck the family, and she knew there was no way for her to go to college. Her mother sold one of their much-needed animals and gave her the money for the train trip to Monmouth. She arrived with fifty cents. Through the generosity of a train depot agent and a college president, she made it through a year of college and obtained her one-year teaching certificate.

She said there were many schools paying $40–$75 for six to seven months of work. She got the a job at Criterion School in Wasco County for $100 plus payment for the janitorial work. She boarded with the family. She had sent a picture with her application with her long hair done-up, but after she was hired she cut her hair. "I arrived to teach and was told I was a wicked woman and not good for the young girls in the community. I stayed, and the most angry laughed about it in later years."

My mother was the last teacher to teach at Criterion in 1925. Today the school is a permanent display at the Oregon State Fairgrounds. She retired in June 1967 from Peterson School in Klamath Falls and passed away in September 1967.

# Planning My Oregon Birthday Party

*Tracy Barry*

*KGW-TV NEWS ANCHOR*

I've been planning a birthday party for our youngest daughter Grace. She wants balloons. Done. Crafts and cake. Easy. Then we got to the guest list. Is it really possible for a child of six to have so many "best" friends? I don't blame her though, since it's friends that make a party fun.

It got me thinking about Oregon's landmark 150th birthday. What a party it would be if we could invite anyone we wanted from history! I am far from an expert on Oregon history, but it's not hard to come up with a long list. I'll get this party started with a few suggestions, and then the guest list is all yours.

Number one on my list is Sacagawea. I love reading about Lewis and Clark, but I so want to know more about what that journey was like for their Native American guide. And if nothing else we could finally settle the name-pronunciation question—is it SAC-a-ja-wea or Sa-COG-a-wea, or something else entirely?

Next up, another woman. American missionary Narcissa Whitman was reportedly one of the first white women to cross the Rocky Mountains with her husband Marcus in 1836. Having read some of her journal and many of her letters home, I feel as though I know her. I admire her courage and faith. She truly loved the Northwest, but the Whitmans' relationship with the local Cayuse and Nez Perce people went from friendly to uneasy, and then worse, during their eleven years here. Both Narcissa and her husband died very violently. The extensive collection of her writings paints a vivid, if sometimes narrow, view of life then. She would be a fascinating party guest.

Just one more: Ing "Doc" Hay, a Chinese herbal doctor who practiced in John Day for more than sixty years. Oregon sure wasn't considered tolerant back then. In 1888, just being Chinese put your life at risk, but he and a friend opened a very successful general store and medical center. His clinic thrived for sixty years offering traditional herbal therapy. It's now the Kam Wah Chung State Heritage Site, complete with more than five hundred herbs that "Doc" left when he died. Many of them haven't been identified. There are so many questions we could ask him.

It's your turn now. Who would be on your guest list? Unlike little Grace, you have no limit.

# The Warner Story

*Fred Warner Sr.*

This story begins in 1863 in Independence, Missouri, during the Civil War. With seven children and loyalties divided between the North and South, the Jenkins family found a solution: sell the farm and head for Oregon, the land of opportunity.

My great-great-grandparents, William and Elizabeth Jenkins, were the leaders of the family. With seventy-five head of livestock, they joined a wagon train and arrived at the Lone Tree Valley in 1864. There they established a homestead in what is today the heart of Baker Valley in eastern Oregon. Nancy Jenkins, my great-grandmother, walked the entire distance at age sixteen, driving the horses and cattle with an older brother. She later married Jonathan Parker, a sheep man from Canada.

They established a cattle ranch eight miles north of Baker City, on the original route of the Oregon Trail. The house that stands on this land today has been our family's home for seven generations. This portion of what is today a larger ranch has always been operated by some member of our family, including my parents, myself, my brother Carl, and my son Fred Jr. It is now owned and operated by my grandson Eric Colton and his wife Darcy. Their two children comprise the seventh generation.

I have lived in Baker Valley my entire life, eighty-two years, with the exception of serving in the U.S. Navy during World War II. After many years of active ranching I now remain connected with the operation. Over the past twenty years, I have devoted time and effort to preserving and protecting the Oregon Trail and its importance to the history of the state of Oregon. I helped establish the National Historic Oregon Trail Interpretive Center on Flagstaff Hill, six miles from Baker City.

I am proud to say that I lived in the same house as a lady who walked the Oregon Trail in 1864, and that I shook the hand of the first man to walk on the moon in 1969. It is my belief that history unrecorded is history lost.

# Millsburg? No Way! We Are West Linn, and We Are Famous for a Rock!

## Cornelia Seigneur

West Linn sits on Willamette Falls, where Native American tribes gathered to fish and live before European settlement in the area. In 1840, Major Robert Moore, age fifty-eight and a colonist from Missouri and Illinois, arrived on the Oregon Trail as a member of the Peoria Party from the state of Illinois. They were among the first pioneers to attempt to create an American colony in Oregon. The Peoria Party set out on May 1, 1839, to colonize the Oregon Country on behalf of the United States, and to force out British fur-trading companies.

Moore purchased title to one thousand acres of land from local Native American inhabitants in 1840. Notably, Moore was one of the few settlers to offer money to the Native Americans for their land. The tribes retained their fishing rights and homes on Moore's land. Moore's platted township was officially named "Robin's Nest" in 1843, and in 1845, the Territorial Legislature of Oregon voted to change Robin's Nest to Linn City in honor of Dr. Lewis Fields Linn, a U.S. senator from Missouri, who was the inspiration for the 1850 Donation Land Claim Act.

Within a few years of arriving, Moore had built flour and lumber mills, along with dwellings for mill workers. Soon there was a chair factory, a tavern, a wagon shop, and a gunsmith. He also fashioned a breakwater and portage basin. By 1860, Linn City had a population of 225, but in 1861, it was partially destroyed by a fire, and then entirely by a flood. It became a "lost city." Willamette Falls continued drawing industry and people, and other small communities were established over the years.

In 1913, a group of mill professionals and managers, who lived in the Bolton and Sunset areas, formed the West Side Improvement Club to discuss incorporating into Oregon, in order to gain tax revenue from the mills and the hydroelectric plant, as well as tracts clustered near the west end of the bridge. They voted in 1913 to incorporate as a city within the state of Oregon, and included the mills as well as Sunset City, West Oregon City, Bolton, Willamette Heights, the west-side addition to Oregon City, Windsor, and Weslynn.

A few representatives from the Crown Columbia Paper Company offered five dollars for the best name for the proposed newly incorporated city in Oregon. Suggestions included: Twilight, Millsburg, Willamette Links, Wiloreton, Belvidere, Firland, Hoodview, Oregon View, Rose City, Rosecliff, Sunnyside, and Westlynn. Millsburg won.

However, no one was satisfied with the name except its author. Using some pioneer-style democracy, on June 28, 1913, the men who sponsored the contest had it announced in the Oregon City *Morning Enterprise* newspaper that Millsburg would be renamed West Linn, in memory of Dr. Lewis Fields Linn and the old pioneer town of Linn City, which had been named after him but was destroyed in 1861.

Incidentally, West Linn is famous for a rock—the Willamette Meteorite, which was discovered in 1902 and sits in New York's American Museum of Natural History—but that's another story.

# A Passage by River

*Constance Spiegel*

Two boys and five adults were afloat on a wide green river, as beautiful and exotic as its Native American name: *Umpqua*. Their trip took them from Roseburg to Gardiner, some eighty miles over many rapids—notably, Sawyer's Rapids at Scottsburg—and on from there to the once-bustling town of Gardiner on the coast.

The mill my grandfather, Frederick Herman Schlegelmilch, and his brother Otto had built in Roseburg had failed, so they sought greener pastures, hoping to find work at the Simpson Mill in Gardiner. The only road available at the time was a hacked-out stage road known to mire its victims axle-deep in mud. They chose to travel by river instead.

Grandpa and his brother Otto built the raft of planks on a gravel bank alongside the river. They and my grandmother Della, their sister "Aunt Jessie," and Miss Bodie, a family friend, left in 1912, possibly in the late summer after a record rainfall in August had swollen the river to navigable size. The two barefoot boys in rolled-up trousers were my Uncle Harold, ten at the time, and his cousin Eugene, who would have been about seven.

Uncle Harold told me the story of the raft trip when he was in his eighties, a decade before he passed away in 1991. He said that the sheriff from Roseburg had ridden up on horseback and had hollered at them to stop because the trip was considered too dangerous—but the warning came too late. They had just taken off. No one had yet made it over the rapids (and one notoriously narrow passage with a ten-foot drop near Scottsburg) in a craft of their size without cracking up.

Uncle Harold remembered great fishing by day and tying up at night to cook over a campfire. One farmer waved them over to share a big, meaty chunk of sturgeon he had just caught. "It was fun!" was how Uncle Harold summed up the experience. As Huck Finn famously says, "You feel mighty free and easy and comfortable on a raft." Well, not exactly. It was cramped and soggy when it rained, and everyone had to stay put in their place.

In Gardiner, Grandpa and Otto did find work, but the women and Harold and Eugene lived out a wet, dreary winter alongside the cannery. The romance was gone, but the journey was just beginning. They rode the stagecoach over the beach to Coos Bay, and eventually booked passage on the steamer Breakwater to Portland, where they settled in 1916.

A few words on the back of an old family album photo got me hooked on this story, and I encourage everyone out there to do the same—you may find a Huck Finn and Tom Sawyer in your family history, too!

*Theresa Sousa*

I am a sixth-generation Oregonian. My great-great-grandfather, Agusta Hickithier, was one of the original founders of Drain. He, Jessie Applegate, and Frank Drain were the first settlers in the area. Jessie moved on after a while and found his way to the Jacksonville area. My great-great-grandfather owned a large ranch and mill just north of Drain. He was also the town barber and photographer.

My great-grandfather, Rufus Beverly Hickithier, used to drive the coal wagon from the train station in Drain to Reedsport twice a month when he was a boy. Later, he took over the mill and ranch. He was interviewed by the historic society in the '70s and told of the time the KKK came to town and called a meeting at the grange hall in Curtin. He said, "Me and Mommie (that's what he called his wife) went up to see what they had to say. We decided it was a bunch of devilment, so we went home."

In later years, he was deaf and couldn't turn his head to the right, and he had a stiff leg. He would still "take a notion" to go to town now and then, so he would sneak off and fire up the truck until he could feel the vibration. This of course would alert Great-grandma May, and she would call Uncle Gene, who was the town officer, to tell him Rufus was coming down off the hill.

Then it was Uncle Gene's job to get down to the intersection—the town's only intersection—and guide traffic. You see, they had put in a traffic light and no one had asked my great-grandfather, so he refused to stop. Now everyone in town—and in Curtin, and Yoncalla—knew to watch out for Rufus, but just in case a stranger was coming though from Reedsport or approaching him from the right, Uncle Gene was there to help. So much more I could tell you. Seven generations of stories!

# Natives

*M.J. Damewood*

We call ourselves natives, with no clear definition of what makes us so. We've been here longer than many. We can remember when that corner used to be this and when that strip mall used to be a meadow. There is a compulsion that motivates our fervent pride. We are the keepers of the stories of this land, and we believe that these stories matter. We may resist perpetual progress and resent certain immigration, but we know that it is inevitable. We are those who hope for a bitter and wet February, a February that drives doubt and despair into our core. Maniacally, we let it mingle within, creating even more native sentiment. It is our trade-off, our penance, for being allowed to take from this land that will call to her all those who seek majesty and wonder.

My sense of being native comes from the north: a French Canadian fur trapper, Joseph DeLore, who settled the Willamette Valley with Mani Luzahn, his Blackfoot bride. They called for a priest, and Father Blanchett remarried them in the first Catholic parish in the Oregon Territory. Settlers followed, and my family moved east, imprinting sagebrush and hot springs and open skies into my bones. The west is home, our first home. The east is our retreat. Wounds garnered in the belly of Oregon's past are not easily healed; they linger in our "nativeness," further proof of our sacrifice for this place.

We carry these stories. We gather them to us, for within them are the hopes of our past. We are all blessed who live in this land, this Oregon.

# Celebrating Our Grandmothers' Journeys to Oregon

*Carla Tomlin Mundt, Laura Mundt, and Tomlin Paolucci*

Naomi Banks was born in Arkansas in 1851 and started west on April 6, 1852, along with a half-sister and a half-brother; her father, Hilkiah Banks; and mother, Martha Jane Sherrod Banks; and her paternal grandparents. They were part of a train of 104 wagons that were headed for the Oregon country.

The Banks family eventually pulled into Oregon City in November 1852, but the trip had its dark times. They buried Grandfather Banks on the bank of the Umatilla River, about four miles from the present Indian reservation, and Grandmother Banks was buried at Burnt River.

In the spring, Hilkiah Banks took his family to Corvallis, where he took up Donation Land Claim NO. 5134. They left the area in 1857 for a donation land claim in the Oakland/Sutherlin area.

The family increased in numbers after reaching Oregon. Three were born in Corvallis, and eight were born in Roseburg. In 1871, Naomi Banks married J. B. Dickenson of Polk County. They moved with their two children to Umatilla County in 1875. They landed on October 10 at Alkali Flats. They farmed eighty acres, raising wheat, and he opened a blacksmith shop at the crossroads about two miles from what is now Athena.

In an interview in 1929, Naomi said there were some stirring times during those early years. Their house was right on the Native American trails, and it was a common thing for Naomi to gather the youngsters in the house and shut and lock the doors if members of the tribes were in sight.

On one occasion a rider came through with the warning that the Native Americans were coming and killing as they came. After days of nervous uncertainty it was decided to go to Fort Walla Walla. They started at night, reaching Milton at about 10 PM The only place to stay was the saloon, so the place was cleaned up and men, women, and children spent the night there.

The women and children were left at Fort Walla Walla, and the men returned to look after the stock. There was a dugout at the Dickenson farm, which the men surrounded with a stockade. Here the farmers of the neighborhood gathered at night with guards.

When asked if there was any hard sledding along the pathway, Mrs. Dickenson replied with a smile: "Well, there were many times when it was pretty hard shucking, and we didn't know where the next sack of flour was coming from, but thank the good Lord, it always came somehow."

# Once Again Bend's Powerhouse:
# Bill Smith and the Old Mill District

*Marie Melsheimer*

In the summer of '69, twenty-nine-year-old William Lee "Bill" Smith
came to Bend. Since then, he has been an instrumental part of shaping
many of the area's landmarks, such as the Old Mill District and Les
Schwab Amphitheater. Over the years, Bill has seen the small logging town
of Bend grow in size, grow in traffic, but also grow in livability.

"Some people focus on the negative aspects of Bend's growth," he
explained, "but it's hard to deny the ways in which growth has contrib-
uted positively to the quality of life in Central Oregon, from restaurants,
to schools, to jobs. When I moved to Bend in 1969, the chances of my
kids finding a good job here were zero. Now, here they are, both working
in Bend."

Bend was founded on the timber industry more than one hundred
years ago, drawing on the huge resource of raw materials in the Deschutes
National Forest. In 1916, two of the world's largest saw mills cropped up on
the banks of the Deschutes River: the Brooks-Scanlon and Shevlin-Hixon
mills. For the next seventy-eight years, the mills and their three soaring
smokestacks dominated Bend's skyline and its economy.

"The most memorable event in Bend's history, in my opinion, was when
the mills ran out of timber," said Smith. "The Forest Service decided to stop
cutting like they had been and turned the economy upside down."

In fact, what had once been a resource for two hundred million board
feet of lumber dwindled down to only two million feet in 1988. "With both
sawmills closed," Smith continued, "Bend was left with a wonderful asset:
the river running through this property. The town grew up around the saw
mill, so we were looking at empty land in the middle of town with a river
running through it, but no way to get there."

With his vision of making the river accessible, he knew that there was a unique opportunity to create something special with this land. After more than five years of planning, Smith's development partners began by restoring 14,000 lineal feet of the river area. The edges of the river—which had been destroyed by floating logs—were restored to create habitat for native creatures, such as fish, mink, otters, and birds.

Bill Smith also honored the site's history by turning three of the original mill buildings into a visual centerpiece for the "new" Old Mill District. Three prominent structures built in 1923—the Fuel Building, the Powerhouse Building, and the Electric Shop—make up the Old Mill District's "powerhouse complex" with its three distinctive smokestacks.

Perhaps one of the most frequented locations in the Old Mill District is the popular five-acre outdoor Les Schwab Amphitheater, which did not receive its name through a company sponsorship by Les Schwab Tire Company, but is actually named after the man himself.

"I don't think of myself as an entrepreneur; Les Schwab was an entrepreneur," Smith said. "He built a huge company that pioneered the concept of sharing profits with employees. I see him as one of my own mentors."

Today, the Old Mill District has a mix of uses and employs more people than the same land did during the height of the timber industry in Bend. It offers retail, dining, office space, and entertainment, as well as residential housing that was built in during the sawmill years.

Bill Smith summed it up best: "Oregon is Oregon because of its diversity. The coast, the mountains, the desert with the swamps in the middle. It has a little bit of everything."

Perhaps one of the best "bits" landed right here in Bend—Bill Smith and the resulting creation of today's Old Mill District.

# Women of the Oregon Trail:
## Francis Burris Tandy Harlow

## Rhonda Gill

Francis Burris Tandy Harlow and her husband, their six children, and her mother, brothers, and sisters all set forth in May of 1850 from Independence, Missouri, on the Oregon Trail, headed for California. There were four Conestoga wagons in their party, as well as one shiny black buggy pulled by four black matching ponies. This was Francis's prized possession. Her husband, a sensible, sturdy man, told her that, if she wanted to take such frills with her, she had to be responsible for them. So, she was. She drove that buggy and ponies herself as far as the edge of the Snake River. They met attacks by native tribes, storms, and floods all along the way, but Francis brought her buggy safely through each crisis.

The Snake River was at full flood capacity by the time they reached it. Francis's sister, Jemima, was riding with her on the buggy, carefully clutching her carpetbag. Her mother had entrusted her to carry the precious family Bible in her bag, and Jemima, at thirteen years of age, had taken the responsibility very seriously. The river swelled as they were crossing, and the buggy tipped. Jemima nearly fell and dropped her bag, and she cried out for help. The wagon train leader, Mr. Jerome B. Greer, called to his dog. The dog jumped into the river and fetched the carpetbag, which was slowly drifting away, and returned it to Jemima. Francis and Jemima were forced to abandon the buggy in the swollen river, where it had become lodged in the muddy bottom, but the ponies were saved, as well as the Bible. Francis now shared her mother's wagon, and she and her sister spent days carefully waving the Bible's pages in the air, drying them one by one.

Today, that same Bible can be seen on display in the First Baptist Church of Eugene, Oregon. Within the pages of that book are dried wildflowers believed to have been gathered by Jemima and the children along the trail.

# The Passenger Train

*Robert C.A. Moore*

In the winter of 1942 our family lived on Northeast 52nd Avenue, about three hundred feet south of the freight rail track that parallels U.S. Highway 30. The rare appearance of passenger trains on the line would capture our attention, and when one appeared we would dash outside to wave and smile at the soldiers heading east.

One Sunday morning the cry, "troop train," brought us to the front porch where we performed our ritual. Some cars into the train my mother said, "I think there are women and children on that train." A few cars later she had figured out who the passengers were. We continued waving and smiling.

A week or so later, my older sister received a postcard from a friend. She was a daughter in one of the Japanese truck farmer families who, until several weeks prior, had been our neighbors. The card noted that our family, waving enthusiastically, had been a positive note for the Japanese-American citizens heading toward war-long confinement.

# Dusty Hoesly

Jakob Hösli, one of my father's ancestors, was a poor Catholic farmer in Glarus, Switzerland. Like many Europeans of his time, unable to feed his family and desperate for hope, and perhaps a victim of Protestant purges, he emigrated to the New World. Anglicizing the family name once he'd arrived in America, from Hösli to Hoesly, Jakob traveled west, settling in New Glarus, Wisconsin, a town filled with other Swiss immigrants. Another of my paternal forebears headed further west at the turn of the twentieth century, this time to Milwaukie, Oregon, where the family home remains today. My grandpa ran a furniture store that included the first elevator in the city, and my grandma, a nurse in a hospice facility, noted that, whatever worldly possessions folks came in with, they all left the same. The Milwaukie Museum on Railroad Avenue features our family history throughout its holdings.

My mother's family traveled from Grand Rapids, Michigan. My great-great-grandfather hopped trains as he traveled to Carus, Oregon, where he built a farmhouse on sixty acres of fertile ground. The cows and hay fields have since been replaced by my uncle's Christmas trees, but our family remains on the land today. Before my grandpa settled onto my grandma's family farm, he was banished in absentia from the AFL for recruiting people to its then-rival, the CIO; arrested in Seattle for inciting a hunger strike; and added to an FBI watch list of suspected communists by J. Edgar Hoover. Once he was married and raising a family on the farm, he became a dispatcher for the Southern Pacific Railroad at Brooklyn Yard and remained active in unions. When he died too young of cancer, my grandma worked at Fred Meyer to feed the family, and the older children helped raise the younger ones.

My family is steeped in Oregon history and territory, mostly in Clackamas County. I love that I grew up near farms and towns where pioneers could make their mark, places an hour-and-a-half away from a desert, beach, mountain, or forest. I grew up valuing the progressiveness of the state that passed the nation's first bottle bill, that turned all beachfront land into public property, and that enacted the Death with Dignity Act. Oregon is also the land of Wayne Morse, who declared his independence from political parties by carrying a folding chair down the aisle of the U.S. Senate chambers in 1953. Oregon is a state where you can tell a true native by his or her opposition to sales taxes, self-serve gas stations, and Californians; a state that mixes ornery individualism with a communitarian spirit; a state that honors hard work well done; and a state where humble people like my ancestors could make a good living and try to change the world.

Modern Oregon

The stories in this chapter embody the uniqueness and diversity
that characterize the people who make up modern Oregon.

# Things We Take for Granted

## Chris Hampton

All my life I have lived here in Oregon. I have been taking the things here for granted for that long as well. The animals that breathe here, the forests that live here, the places we live. I have been so desensitized to my surroundings I hardly notice them anymore. Sometimes I have to stop and slow down a while before I see or hear the things that our amazing state has to offer.

The diversity of this state's geography is different from that of any other state in America—dry deserts in the east; wet, stormy beaches in the west. The mountainous terrain in the south is much different from the Willamette Valley in the north. There are day-to-day glories that most people living here just overlook because they have seen them a million times over.

Even the weather is ever-changing—snowing one minute, raining the next, and then sunshine here and there. Most of the time, though, it's raining. The cities we live in and visit are also different. You'll be traveling though the urban, crowded streets of Portland one minute, and then, if you take Highway 99 south, you'll hit the small suburb of Gladstone, leaving it as quickly as you came. You'll then pass the town of Oregon City, and if you decide to continue onward, you'll reach the rural area of Canby. This can all be done in half an hour.

The point I am trying to make is that people don't treasure the area we live in the same way. We go on with our day-to-day lives without even pausing for a moment to appreciate the state we live in.

# My Oregon

*Dorothy Heath*

For ninety years, I've lived in Oregon and called it home. I was born May 28, 1918, on south Sixth Street in Marshfield. I lived there for many years, and my plan was to spend the rest of my life there, but an unexpected operation caused me to change my address. I currently live in Ocean Ridge in Coos Bay, and I remain loyal to our lovely state.

Why do I love Oregon? It meets all of my needs. I'm a lover of beauty. The ocean scenery has a special appeal with all her many moods—storming, sunny, calm, and wild. She is second to none. She dresses like a beautiful queen in all her splendor. The azure blue of our Pacific Ocean with its many birds—pelicans, sand pipers, and various gulls—provides a crown for this queen of states.

As I walk barefoot on the beach admiring the cliffs sculpted by the pounding, restless waves of the sea, all of my problems seem less important. Like sand sifting through my hands, problems will get lost as the day passes.

The area gets darker. Brilliant red and gold streaks the sky. All of the rainbow's colors are in a beautiful sunset. The sky makes a display like a piece of heaven; God is good to Oregon. The sunset continues to change until the glory of the sky slips behind the horizon beyond the sea. The afterglow continues until darkness melts it away.

Oregon has been blessed with everything good. The sea is my Oregon. My roots go deep, and I'm glad that my family chose this place as their home. I hope to make it to the century mark here in my Oregon.

# In Tune with Ourselves and
# Our Environment

## *Dawn Rasmussen*

As a non-native Oregonian transplanted almost twenty-five years ago to this incredible state, I've grown accustomed to thinking about everything I do in a green way since setting foot here. From recycling or composting as much waste as possible, to not consuming as much, to consciously thinking about how I am going to connect various errands so I reduce my driving (and subsequent carbon footprint), it's a green way of thinking. I probably wouldn't have adopted this perspective if I had stayed in any of my previous residences in Wisconsin, North Carolina, or Louisiana. It's a different mentality in those states. To me, Oregon's forward thinking is completely cutting-edge, and is producing some of the technology that will provide power and resources for future generations. The Green Revolution is starting right here with the explosion of renewable energy companies, recycling programs, connections to local producers, and mass transit. And it is extremely exciting to be at the heart of all of this enterprise.

Maybe this evolution of thinking has a lot to do with the hordes of outdoor enthusiasts (I count myself among them) who are out in nature in all seasons, reveling in nature's majesty. Being in the outdoors brings you closer to environmental impacts. I've seen a profound respect and awareness for our environment here and how it impacts us. This is shaping what we do now on a daily basis, and how we will live in years to come.

Out of this environmental awareness has also come a sense of responsibility. I can tell you that there is one secret spot that I enjoy visiting in eastern Oregon, far up in the vast folds of a wilderness area, where the only sound you'll hear is the wind soughing in the tops of the mountain pines and the occasional birdcalls. It is peaceful, serene, and ageless, without disruption from humans.

That, to me, is the sound of infinity, and as stewards of this great state, it is ever so important for us to protect and preserve this, not just for future generations, but for the planet as well. Will development ever touch this region, I wonder? I sure hope not. These isolated pockets of undisturbed natural landscape may play an even greater role in the future health of the planet than we might now suspect.

I spend a lot of time in reflection while visiting these sacred remote areas, thinking about how I can do a better job of being a caretaker of this planet. I feel grateful that Oregon has taken giant leaps forward to instill in every citizen a sense of responsibility. Little things add up to big things, and that's where momentum begins.

Others from outside the area may scoff at the "greenie" Oregonians, but if they look a little closer, they will realize that there's a reason why we want to protect this precious resource. It's our living room. Our dinner table. Our vacation spot. Our livelihood. Our home.

I predict that there will be a day when gasoline will be a faded memory, and the days of supermarkets being chock-full of vegetables and products from around the world will seem the epitome of excess and gluttony. We currently take this for granted, not really factoring in the distance a vegetable from California or a bottle of wine from Chile had to travel in order to reach our local grocery store shelf. Understanding how intertwined our commerce is with transportation systems will help us plan for the future of our state, our nation, and our planet. As economic conditions fluctuate and businesses go boom or bust, it is also important for us to take individual responsibility to do better despite external market forces: Use more efficiently. Buy less. Be innovative. Demand technologies that will help us be less wasteful. It's not just an economic condition, but an environmental one too, as global climate change continues to shift weather patterns and alter our environment forever.

Oregon is home to an amazing blend of rural and urban landscapes, scenic beauty, and diverse peoples. It's also a hotbed of ideas, can-do innovation, and a careful concern for others and the environment. I feel lucky to be part of an amazing community that is getting in tune with its surroundings and taking steps to protect them—for all of our sakes.

# Strangers on Unfamiliar Ground

*Nancy Murphy*

We had little in common. I was eighteen and new to Oregon, having taken the phrase "Go west, young man" to heart. Nevermind I was a girl—I'd looked forward to 1971 and coming of age for a long time. Sam was over eighty, a native Oregonian living in a nursing home against his will. He'd come of age long ago and had no future left to speak of.

"Beware," the head nurse told us the morning he was admitted. "He hits and bites. Swears and spits. Don't try to handle him alone."

I'd left the idea of heeding advice back in upstate New York, so when I was assigned his room, I went alone to serve him breakfast.

He took one look at me and spat. "Untie my damn hands," he raged. "I'm not an animal."

I sized up the situation. He had refused to eat in the last facility he'd been in. "Okay," I said. "But you have to let me help you with breakfast."

I took his grunt as agreement and freed his hands.

Immediately, he lashed out, upending his tray. Eggs and juice flew into the air, much of it landing on me.

Eyes fierce, he cursed me.

I stood my ground and swore back.

"You've got a nasty mouth for a little girl," he said.

"Not as bad as yours."

I called for another breakfast, saying I'd spilled this one. I didn't put his restraints back on. I doubt he'd appreciate my efforts, but at least he knew I wasn't like everyone else. I'd even fib if I thought it was for the greater good.

Sam became my reason to come to work. I could empathize with his anger at being under someone else's control. Wasn't that why I'd come to Oregon myself? To be my own person? Eventually he let me push his wheelchair around the nursing home. He stopped hitting people and no longer had to be restrained. I couldn't say he liked me, and he never initiated any conversations, but at least he answered simple questions without swearing.

A couple of days before Christmas, snow flurries teased me with hopes of a white Christmas. Homesickness had been nipping at my faith in my ability to make it on my own, and I thought this connection with my past might ease that some. But at the end of my shift, when I went into Sam's room to say goodbye, gloom descended.

Finding Sam's eyes closed, I moved to the window. The snow had all but melted, and the landscape was bleak and gray. Tears rolled down my cheeks unchecked.

I jumped as Sam's voice broke the silence. "Look at the way the snow melts and makes little rivers out there," he said. "It's almost like being in the wilderness. It's beautiful, don't you think?"

I turned to him, brushing my tears away. Compassion had restored life to his expression. Our eyes met, and a silent understanding far deeper than I'd experienced with anyone before passed between us. We knew nothing of each other's history, had no common friends, had never shared our feelings or thoughts with each other, but in that moment, we recognized we were all either of us had.

And it was enough.

# *Bruce* Tucker

I am a field agent with the Department of Revenue, where I've worked since 1982. Because of my experience, supervisors asked me to go from North Bend to Medford to train a new employee, Janice, in May 2007. We'd never met before this.

As we talked during the week, we discovered that our lives had only a few degrees of separation that had begun more than half a century earlier. She mentioned that her family came from Oklahoma, and moved to Sweet Home, Oregon, in the late '40s. I thought that was an interesting coincidence, as my mother was born in Oklahoma, as were my wife Mary's parents. I asked her what town her family had lived in. She told me Broken Bow. That really got my attention, because my in-laws moved from Broken Bow to Sweet Home in the late '40s, too. Broken Bow is a tiny community virtually unknown outside southeastern Oklahoma. (It will, however, achieve a modicum of fame in the future, when a Klingon shuttle will crash into a cornfield in Broken Bow, and humans will encounter Klingons for the first time, at least according to the premiere episode of *Star Trek Enterprise.*)

When I talked to Mary, she talked to her mother and called me back. She told me that her parents and Janice's parents had been friends and frequently spent time playing cards at each other's homes. We then realized that Janice and Mary were both born in Lane Mack hospital in Sweet Home—not your major medical megalopolis—and that the same doctor delivered them. Then to cap it all off, we found out that my father-in-law and Janice's uncle were friends when they were kids. As ornery eight-year-olds, they were throwing rocks, and Janice's uncle threw a rock that put out my future father-in-law's eye, giving him a whole new outlook on life. At that point, the Disney song "It's a Small World After All" invaded my brain. It returns every time I talk to Janice. We have made a vow not to throw rocks at each other.

# Three Muses Found on Mount Hood

*Scot Siegel*

*"The language of landscape is mute and immaculate"*
— Charles Wright

Dear young wife,

On the washed-out plain called guys'
weekend in the mountains
I place atop the cairn rising from glacial till
for you one river stone from the valley.

Dear teenage daughter,

What you do not say aloud this year
I hear cached in talus on the northern slopes
little hearts like mismatched socks; flox & lupine
clutched on the moonscape.

Dear youngest daughter, fellow poet.

I think of you under your sheets hiding,
a storm of your own making
building outside your window
on wings of lenticular clouds, like bats'
dreams tug our tents, yours & mine
from afar…

Yes, we are geologists, you and I.
We fill our pockets with carnelian agates
& less beautiful specimens: clam shells,
split & riddled by sea lice; false-fossils
bits of iron slag we haul in t-shirt
rucksacks from the shoreline; we keep
such things like talismans to ward-off
nightmares and stranger premonitions...

We care for these objects like brittle birds
the way I care for these words, little glass
origami I carry down the mountain to tell you
someday

# Fifth Generation Oregonian

*Jennifer Larson*

I'm a fifth-generation Oregonian and proud of it! I'll never forget that Christmas Day when all five generations were able to have our photo taken together. Grammy was so proud to have her daughters, granddaughter, and great-granddaughter all together that year.

When I was nineteen and freshly married, we had to move away to find work. We ended up in Reno, Nevada, and hated every minute of it. Reno has two seasons: summer and winter. That's it. We missed Oregon so much we took out the Oregon map; said, "Let's get out of here;" closed our eyes; and pointed. My finger landed between Roseburg and Eugene. We decided on Eugene since it was a college town. It would be hip and happening for us young folks. Ha! It was the best move we've ever made, and we will retire here. We will never leave Oregon. How could we? We have the best of everything: ocean, rivers, mountains, volcanoes, and desert. Oh, and don't forget the seasons. We have all four of them. Enjoy!

# Taking Oregon with Me

## Jeannine Jordan

I moved to Oregon from the flat, treeless plains of Kansas, so the awesome majesty of Oregon's towering Douglas firs made a powerful first impression. I came to study organ and harpsichord at the University of Oregon. Not having the funds at the time for a pipe organ of my own, I opted instead for a handcrafted instrument of the harpsichord family—a virginal. The builder I chose for this delicate and artful instrument had many questions regarding details, but the one question that caused me to pause was, "What design or image do you want painted on the soundboard?"

I pondered the decision about the soundboard painting for a long time. The painting on the soundboard of one's personal instrument traditionally tells something of its owner—something of her passions, her dreams, her inspiration. Knowing that graduate school was ending soon and the prospect of staying in this place of beauty and inspiration was not probable, I decided to give my virginal a lasting impression of the Oregon I had quickly come to love. I had a powerful yet delicate Douglas fir painted onto the soundboard. This was the image of Oregon I was to take with me.

Yes, I did leave Oregon. My virginal with its Douglas fir accompanied me to the cornfields of Iowa. There it reminded me of the inspiration of Oregon until finally, the two of us came home to make music here again.

# Culture Shock

*Melissa Smart*

The first time I understood that the fifty states are not created equal was while I was in my early twenties, when I went to visit a friend in a Rocky Mountain state. We were having lunch in a cafeteria. I finished my pop and asked her, "Where do I put my pop can?"

"The trash is over there," she replied.

I couldn't comprehend this, so I rephrased the question, "No, I mean, where is the recycling?"

"Oh," she said, "we don't have that. Just put it in the trash."

I was dumbfounded! I looked around and saw a sea of people, all of whom were throwing aluminum cans in the garbage. Such a wanton waste of resources! Such disregard for the environment!

This was many years ago, and I imagine much remains unchanged. I had to leave Oregon to fully understand how "ahead of our time" we are. God bless Oregon.

# My Mountains

## Lisa Jacoby

Baker City became my home on May 9, 1979. It was just "Baker" then, and to this day I still drop the "City." You always know a newcomer because they insist on "Baker City." (The town was originally Baker City, then was Baker until 1990 when it was returned to the former name.)*

I graduated from high school in 1998 and headed to college at Boise State University in Boise, Idaho. Here's the thing about Boise: there are no mountains. Hills, yes, but the horizon stretches on and on and on, and the mountains are very distant. In Baker Valley, we're hemmed in by two mountain ranges—the Elkhorns and the Wallowas. I grew up with these mountains. I've fished in their lakes and hiked their trails.

Living in Boise, a mere two hours to the east, meant I could come home any weekend I wished. I'd hit the road and breathe a sigh of relief when I left traffic behind and drove past the rolling sagebrush hills west of Ontario. Then, right at the exit for a place called Pleasant Valley, I'd turn a gentle corner and would be awarded the most magnificent view of the Elkhorns. I especially love winter, when snow covers the crags and makes the terrain look so rugged. That range rises as you get closer to Baker, and once in town you can see the Wallowas a bit farther away but still just as pretty.

I'd spend the weekend, then climb in my car to head back to Boise. That's when I dreaded that Pleasant Valley corner, because I'd get my last glimpse of the Elkhorns in the rearview mirror before the range disappeared from sight until my next trip home.

I returned to Baker after earning a degree and now live, work, and play in this place that will always be my hometown. My daughter, Olivia, was born in the same hospital as I, and at two weeks of age took a tour around Anthony Lake. She's been all over the Elkhorns, thanks to a backpack and her dad's strong legs. She loves to be outside, and from her earliest age the swaying trees could calm her crankiness.

I never thought I took my mountains for granted, but it took time away to really appreciate my home. I am an Oregonian and never value my state more than when I travel elsewhere.

And I always come back.

*Editors' Note: The town was founded as Baker City in 1870, and the name was changed to Baker in 1911.

# The Skate Scene

## Geo Teodoro

The skate scene in Oregon is great because of all the new skate parks designed by Dreamland Skateparks. The local skate scene started in 1991 with Dreamland's Burnside Park, located in Portland under the Burnside Bridge. After that beginning, Dreamland designers started building other parks around Oregon. Oregon is home to some of the best skate parks in the world, and to some of the most hardcore skate pros. I have had the honor to skate a couple of the Dreamland designs, and I love the way they flow.

My skateboarding days started in seventh grade when I heard that the Lincoln City skate park was trying to get a new pool. I thought the idea for a swimming pool being used for skateboarding was badass, because the sound the skateboard trucks make when they crunch the pool coping just makes me so motivated to shred.

I think I have an advantage over other skaters around the world because I have the best parks around my 'hood. I also think Oregon is cool because so many pros live in this wonderful state. Although Oregon's seasons are rather wet, I still manage to get some skating in year-round. Winter is the worst time to skate because of how rainy and foggy it gets on the coast, but it doesn't stop me.

# Oregon, You Are My Home
# (Original Folksong)

*Suzanne Chimenti*

I teach music at Fairview Elementary School, and I wrote this song for my students. It was recorded by my band, The Mighty Filberts (known for our original Oregon songs). We were joined by a chorus of my students.

OREGON, YOU ARE MY HOME © 2007

Mountains that beckon to heaven
Oceans with emerald foam.
Rivers that roar on the green valley floor
Oregon, you are my home

CHORUS:
You are my home,
You are my home
Rivers that roar on the green valley floor
Oregon, you are my home

The pioneers came for your beauty
Your prairies, the Indians roamed
There's desert sand to the east of your land
Oregon, you are my home

CHORUS

Eagles fly through your canyons
And soar over volcano domes
Salmon swim free on their way to the sea
Oregon, you are my home

CHORUS

Oregon, you are my homeland
and no matter where else I roam
My heart will be near your evergreen trees
Oregon, you are my home.

# Getting Over the Blues

*Janet Dodson*

Pack up the family wagon and hit the trail for La Grande, in Oregon's northeast corner. Pioneers traveling on the Oregon Trail raved about the beauty of the area. They rested in the shadow of the Blue Mountains and restored their strength for the most challenging part of their journey—the climb over the Blues. But after making the climb, they continued westward to the famous Willamette Valley.

Then, gold was discovered in the Blue and Wallowa Mountains. With the mines providing a new market for their products, the rich Grande Ronde Valley soil and climate predicted fortune to industrious farmers. Some pioneers realized what they had missed and came back to settle this fertile valley.

Small towns sprang up around the valley, and roads connected them with farms and mines. Later, the railroad closed the gap between rural and urban Oregon. The hum of activity never died down. The valley remains one of the most productive in Oregon, growing everything from cherries and apples to mint, grass seed, and hay. La Grande became a center for commerce, services, transportation, industry, medicine, education, and government.

Today's visitors don't feel they are stepping back in time—all modern conveniences are readily available—but they often experience a touch of nostalgia. People are friendly. Art and music are bountiful. There is pride in heritage and a strong sense of place. This is what it feels like to have a hometown.

The surrounding mountains provide outstanding outdoor recreation and scenery. The Hells Canyon All-American Road is one of the nation's premier scenic byways. There are plenty of trails for hiking, biking, and backpacking in Oregon's largest national forest and wilderness area. People who prefer motorized transport find the winding back roads and ATV trail systems inviting.

Residents of Union County love parades, and there are many opportunities to watch or participate in them. Every small town has a festival to celebrate what makes that community unique, and while beauty may be in the eye of the beholder, most visitors find much to love about the setting and character of them all. From Crossing the Blues in La Grande to the Union Grassroots Festival, the North Powder Huckleberry Festival, the Cove Cherry Fair, the Elgin RiverFest, and Imbler's Fourth of July, the abundant entertainment, food, and crafts give residents and visitors plenty to smile about.

Union County is also home to two long-running professional rodeos, a variety of other western events, and an active polo club, with one of only three regulation-size fields in Oregon.

While wagons, beasts of burden, and stagecoaches transported whole households 150 years ago, you can get here much more quickly on Interstate 84. Plan to stay a while. You'll discover why many people want to put down roots and never leave.

# Dundee, Oregon, 2009: One Stoplight and Three Gourmet Restaurants

## Susan Sokol Blosser

*Founder, Sokol Blosser Winery*

When Bill Blosser and I settled in the Dundee Hills to start a vineyard, Dundee was a one-street farm town, and the hills on its north side were dotted with prune, filbert, walnut, and cherry orchards. A big nut dryer and a retail sales room full of local fruit specialties, like nuts and prunes, lined the main street, along with the post office, the fire department, the elementary school, the Dundee Women's Club, two gas stations, a small grocery, a truck stop café, and a tavern.

We were among a small group of young couples who thought the Dundee Hills would be the perfect place to plant Pinot Noir grapes and start wineries. David and Diana Lett came first, followed by the Eraths, then us, the Fuquas, and the Mareshes. The idea spread, and in the 1990s an Associated Press writer labeled Dundee "the epicenter of Oregon Pinot Noir." By 2009, the Dundee Hills had become a monoculture of vineyards, with few of the old orchards in sight, and the town had evolved to accommodate its new status.

The same busy state highway, 99w, still ran through the center of town, so the main street was bisected by a steady stream of vehicles, from semis to limos. Talk of a bypass, which would route through-traffic around the town, had flourished for years, but every step forward met with enough opposition to thwart any progress. The stoplight installed at the school corner only exacerbated the situation, as the mix of wine tourists, casino-goers, and coast traffic clogged the road.

Remnants of the old farm life disappeared. The nut dryer, which had been the dominant feature in town, was converted into Argyle Winery, with the adjacent Victorian home refurbished as a tasting room and offices. The buildings along the railroad track, belonging to Westnut Filbert Company, became Twelfth and Maple, a custom-crush wine facility. The two little gas stations gave way to one very large one with a mini-market. The old-fashioned post office and city hall both moved to new, larger quarters off the main street. But the volunteer fire department was still in the middle of town, with the fire trucks visible to passers-by; the Riteway Meat Company still advertised its mobile slaughtering services and its five-foot pepperoni; and the Dundee Women's Club building and the old church remained.

While farming is no longer as evident, vineyards constitute a vital part of the Dundee Hills. The tourist side of wineries has affected the town, which has slowly started to cater to the wine-touring public. Dining has been the biggest change. How many one-street towns can boast three white-table-cloth restaurants? The old Nite Hawk Café reinvented itself as an expensive restaurant called Tina's, and the leap from truck stop to gourmet restaurant symbolizes how Dundee has changed to meet the needs of the times. Tina's, Red Hills Provincial, and the Dundee Bistro, all on the main street within a few blocks of each other, arose to meet the culinary demands of the wine lovers.

As Oregon celebrates its 150 years of statehood, Dundee stands between its past and its future—it still has a main street of less than a mile, with one stoplight and three gourmet restaurants. We're stuck in traffic, but eating well.

# Blazing a Trail to Oregon

*Laural Porter*

KGW-TV NEWS ANCHOR

When my husband and four children and I moved to Oregon, we felt like we were following the Oregon Trail.

Our car had broken down in the middle of nowhere, and we were stranded waiting for a tow truck. Once our van was hooked up to the tow truck, it was more than a hundred-mile drive to the nearest town. The road was dusty and hot, and it felt as if we'd never get there. Nearly twenty-four hours later, we had purchased a new car, hitched our overflowing U-Haul trailer to it, and continued our cross-country journey.

The pioneers, 150 years ago, had a much rougher road. However, I imagine their joy at seeing the sight of the Gorge, Multnomah Falls, and their final destination was very similar to ours. We were finally at our new home, and what a beautiful place it was.

In the many years since then, my children have embraced all that is Oregon. They love camping and skiing, and running in Forest Park. Their favorite family vacations are either skiing at Mount Bachelor or going to the coast. My youngest daughter skis every weekend at Mount Hood with her high school ski team. My eldest daughter says her perfect afternoon is spending hours reading in Powell's Books and having coffee and dessert at a local coffeehouse. My son is an avid Blazer fan, and we all cheer for the Ducks and the Beavers.

As a mother, my dream is that Oregon will always be the place my children call home. I hope they will forever feel that sense of contentment and pride when they arrive back in Oregon after being away for a while. I dream that Oregon can offer my children and all other children affordable housing, good health care, high-paying jobs, and an environment that is clean and beautiful. I dream that their children will believe that Oregon is the best place to live, because we charted a brave and passionate course that was inspired by the first Oregon trailblazers 150 years ago. Happy 150th Oregon!

# Judy Rice

I sit here at my computer trying to write something about a place where my family has lived for five generations. There are over fifteen members of our family buried in the Oswego Pioneer Cemetery.

I can remember when Lake Oswego was just plain Oswego. All the kids in town went to one grade school. We had no school bus service, and the big kids went to Portland to attend Lincoln High. The new (now old) high school was built when I was in seventh grade, and even the seventh and eighth graders went there. We spent our summer days swimming in the lake or at the city pool, then went to the ice cream store and got cones for five cents. We would spend Saturday afternoons at the movies, watching a serial and lots of cartoons for a quarter. What a great time it was to be young!

The town has changed along with the rest of the world, but it is still home. We had our Lake Oswego High fifty-year reunion this year.

On February 14, 1959, I married my wonderful husband. It was the day that the state of Oregon was one hundred years old. This year we are celebrating our fifty years together, along with the state of Oregon, and we have always lived right here close to where I grew up. We have visited every corner of this wonderful state, and we find each place we visit to be a grand new adventure.

# My Life on a Farm

*Nolan Coulter*

I live in Toledo, Oregon. The small town is a community of loggers and mill workers at Georgia Pacific. My family members are hunters. We like to fish for trout in the Siletz River, and the Big Elk Creek, in Harlan.

In the summer, we hay in hot, dusty fields on my grandpa's farm. We use bandannas to cover our faces, and buck the bails on the trailer. When we are done, we drive off back to the farm to unload the hay into the barn. Sometimes we go to the Big Elk to cool off. But, most often, we come home to barbecue on the briquette grill. We cook steak, ribs, and all kinds of finger-licking goodness. After we eat, we sit by the fire and burn wood that we've gathered from our property. We sit out for a long time talking and relaxing. Then we go back inside and go to sleep.

On those days, I feel like I have accomplished something. I worked Oregon's land with my muscles and body. I know it will all grow back next spring.

# From Ten to Sixty in No Time Flat

## Ron Allen

Our parents loaded my three brothers, our older sister, and me into our 1957 Ford station wagon and headed for the world's largest log cabin, also known as the Forestry Building in Portland. It was 1959, I was ten years old, and Oregon was celebrating its centennial. It's difficult to believe that I'll turn sixty this month just as Oregon turns 150. The Portland zoo moved to their new Washington Park location that same year, and Rosy the Elephant was the star attraction. My siblings and I purchased a few trinkets that we swore we would keep forever. Dad said they could be valuable some day.

Well, those souvenirs have long since vanished, the grand old Forestry Building burned to the ground in 1964, and Rosy the world famous elephant is gone also. The memories of our family driving from our home in Hillsboro to the big city of Portland to celebrate our state's one hundredth year will remain with me until I too am gone.

My family and I now live in Forest Park, just minutes from the Oregon Zoo, and of course I've seen lots of changes around here in the last fifty years. So what do I plan to do on Valentine's Day/Oregon's 150th celebration? Load my wife and kids into my car and take them to the zoo to see Rose Tu and find them some sesquicentennial souvenirs that will probably be lost in time, as well as some memories that hopefully will not.

My kids will no doubt be here to celebrate Oregon's bicentennial. I can only imagine what the world will be like in 2059. I just hope that my children's life in Oregon is as pleasant as mine has been for the first sixty years.

# Superslime

*Tim Leigh*

It was my tenth day on the Point Adams Cannery dock in Hammond, Oregon. I stood on a wood riser on the far side of the long, heavy butcher-bench, my feet in knee boots crusted with fish scales, my middle wrapped in a once-white oilcloth apron, my hands in wet cotton gloves. I was holding a stubby knife and reaching for headless, finless fish carcasses that were shooting through a hole in the table bulkhead and stacking up like cordwood. Water splashed out of the workstation faucet, off the fish, and all over me.

"Git movin'," somebody growled. "Ya gotta keep up with the butcher across from ya."

I was a slimer. It was a new guy's job, one all the college kids got. I scraped blood, errant entrails, skin parasites, and slime from the bodies of just-butchered salmon and tuna fish, cleaning them for the canning process in the adjacent buildings on the shore. It wasn't hard work, except for the part where I had to split the spine to clean out the dorsal aorta, but it was cold, and dirty, and it never stopped.

Not your living room.

A portal to the culture of the river cannery dock it was, too. Dark buildings sat sullenly on rows of log pilings about 120 yards into the Columbia River. We walked (or drove) out there on high, planked scaffolds that creaked. Once through the huge rolling door at the entry end, illumination dimmed, which was surprising because there wasn't an interior to speak of. Though the icehouse and main fish handling areas were covered, nothing much else was. There were no windows, just holes in the walls. No drains or refuse containers, just holes in the floor. Fish heads and fins lay about randomly (and routinely). Water ran everywhere, floors were constantly wet and slippery, and salt was sometimes scattered to improve footing. The only warmed area was a small coffee room where crews went for ten-minute breaks at 10:00 and 2:00. Boats moored on the inside of the dock away from the current, off-loading their catches in big boxes and taking on ice from an immense, howling ice-grinding machine.

It was an old-time male place—smelly, brawny, noisy, often dangerous, and it had remained unchanged for decades. It was colored by people like Bill Anderson, the dock boss and carpenter; Clarey Dreyer and Jimmy Kerno, the launch captains; Shorty Rogers, the founder's son and icehouse chief; Monzie Brummet, who talked fast and drove a slow ex-milk truck; Bill Broderick, a brawler with a mysterious, violent past—prison, they said; Pat Broderick, Bill's huge, noisy nephew; Short George Anderson, who chewed snooce and liked to talk low in your ear; and Smitty, the lead butcher who tested his knife edge by shaving his arm. "When hair jumps a coupla inches, yer blade's right," he'd say.

These guys watched to see how you held up, often openly voicing their doubt that you could. They worked hard themselves, but their expectations of prissy college boys were low. I liked them right off, maybe because they were so openly themselves, maybe because their world—a small slice by anybody else's standards—was enough for them.

It was a rite of passage, all right, and I wanted to win approval, I guess. Today was as good a day as any. I'd watched and learned; I was ready. I didn't say anything to anybody; I just lined up the rolling fish bin off my right elbow, sharpened my knife more than usual, and started grabbing fish. Silvers.

Grip the ventral fin flap, thumb under. Sweep the knife down the fish, one swipe. Wrist-flip and swipe the other side. Wrist-flip back. Open and press any blood toward the backbone with the broad of the blade, both sides. Slash down the backbone toward the tail. Turn the knife and return once, scraping the dorsal groove clean. Done.

Heave the fish back to the right without looking. Wham, into the bin. Reach for another and do it again. Faster this time.

"Hey! Yeah, you."

Before very long, Smitty the butcher came around the table wondering where all his fish were going—down the guts hole? "Looks like I'm doin' nothin'," he muttered.

Next, the dock boss stomped up, telling me to stop—he wanted to check my fish. Looked through most the whole bin, but only found one I had to work on more.

And finally, Short George, a professional slimer, leaned over and said, through tobacco juice, "Hey kid, put that damn knife down. It's break time."

I took my apron off and walked into the steamy coffee room, which smelled like fish had been cooked onto its walls, making the proffered coffee and muffin seem less than appetizing. All the butchers and other slimers were sitting on chairs, sipping hot joe, quiet, looking at me. After a long, nerve-jangling minute, Clarey Dreyer spoke up for the group. "Thinkin' of makin' this dock a career, boy? Slime so fast us butchers can't keep up? Makin' us look slack? Nobody ever did that 'fore you got here. What's yer name?"

"Tim," I said, kind of defensively.

"Naw, that ain't it," he said, sweeping his arms in broad maritime gestures. "Fellas, this here is Superslime. He's makin' history. Give him a hand."

Two sarcastic claps, a grunt, and mercifully the recital—and the coffee break—was over. But you know, as long as I worked at Point Adams Packing Company there in Hammond, Superslime was my name.

*Sid Gustafson*

After my folks divorced and my dad flew the coop to Astoria to work on a fishing boat, my sister and I rode the bus out to spend the summer with him—a twenty-hour trip from Big Timber, Montana. Well, we were on the same bus anyway—she was one of those geeks who wanted to sit in the front, and did. Not me; I wasn't that type. Of course we fought over it. She thought she was my boss, but she couldn't make me stay up front with her—no way—and I told her so. Pretty soon I think she preferred me in the back. So there I sat, in the very back row, next to the toilet. I got to inspect everyone who took refuge in the can, and study their toilet habits. The congealed odor of all the nasty things men do to ease the pain of living settled into me on that ride. All the depravity in the world flushed down that toilet, all the way to Oregon, with me not two feet from it all. In Post Falls, an Idaho couple got on and went in the toilet together as the bus lumbered over the nuclear nothingness of eastern Washington.

When we got to Oregon our dad wasn't at the bus station, and by that time Sis and I truly hoped he would be there. My dad was a Vietnam vet and a drug addict. I guess it was a rough war—he never seemed over it. It didn't feel like he cared that much for us, but he probably did. He mostly worried about himself. He whined a lot; that's why mom distanced herself from him. But that's just the way he was, and even I smoke the stuff myself once in a while. I can see how someone with a worried soul might get addicted. It does take things away, especially that sticky Oregon greenbud. Anyway, we spent the summer in Astoria. I can't say we spent it with our father, because he was never really there. We were near him though, and that turned out to be important.

I got a job at Fort Clatsop, a rebuilt fort that was supposed to reconstruct Lewis and Clark's stay at the mouth of the Columbia River two centuries ago. I was in charge of cleaning the latrines and tidying up after all the gawkers who showed up and bought woven rain hats at the curio shop. My sister waited tables in town at the Vegan Café, an earth-pilot setup where the pretty people ate broccoli omelets to chip away at their hangovers.

Occasionally I got to run the admissions booth when the employees in charge went off into the woods to smoke spleef and check on the psilocybin hatch. It must have been the weather in Astoria that created the need for everyone to carry themselves away, all that drenched grey. When I was put in charge, I let everyone in free, unless I didn't like their attitude—then I charged double, and occasionally got called on it by some of the more attentive tightwads. I didn't make much dough at Fort Clatsop, but Sis made good money at the restaurant with her tips. I did learn some important things working there, though—like the fact that every last Clatsop Indian had been exterminated by my ancestors. Not one left today.

One day the sheriff came to get me in a heavy, flat rain. He told me Dad was lost at sea, that he fell out of the fishing boat while shrimping in a squall. Sis cried for two days till Mom showed up. That afternoon, before driving back to Montana, we three sat on a friend's porch and watched the Columbia River mushroom all the crap from America into the sea. Foghorns wrenched their horrid sound over the water and tightened our sorrow. Seals we couldn't see yarped back at our sobs—seals swimming with the souls of the drowned. There never was a funeral; there was no body. It's a good thing, because I might have believed he was dead. But he's not, you know. Dad was a good swimmer—a Navy Seal. Besides, the rum-soaked captain of the boat stopped by that day and told me Dad was wearing a lifejacket when he went overboard. That night I had a dream that Pa made it to shore and ran away from a life he couldn't handle, ran away to a safer place.

It all happened twenty-three years ago. Every time I ride a bus it's like I'm on a field trip to find him. And I still ride in the back.

## Warren Hartung

I am green,
I was born so
Within the womb of Oregon,
Not so special, really
But unique enough
To know my heritage
My Oregon is a part of me...
Yes, I have traveled,
And lived in other places
But never was at home
Until I found my way
Back down the throat
Of this vast and lush river gorge
And felt her closing in around me...
Saw the windswept might
Of the Columbia,
And felt the coolness
Of tall green conifers
Comfort me,
Felt the tribal tears
For days long lost,
And held open my heart
To those who have
Traveled before me,
Yet always returning here
Always returning home...

# Oregon Country Fair: That's How I Live

*India Powell*

Each year, as I arrive at the Oregon Country Fair and proceed to sit in my car for an indefinite amount of time, waiting to be directed to a parking lot, I can't help but feel as if I'm home. All the familiar ingredients in that OCF elixir seem to beckon me onward: the friendly painted faces, the hay bales, the international cuisine, the solar ovens, and everything in extreme. Every year brings a new adventure, but it is always characterized by the same elements.

Walking in through the front gate, I am inevitably greeted by the customary scene: families, draped in hemp clothing, fervently run amok while setting up their booths; the lady at the ticket desk wildly waves her purple feather boa as she yells like a carnival barker to the next person in line; and then there's the man who casually walks down the dirt path wearing nothing but a lanyard on his groin.

For one glorious weekend, anything goes. I am free to behave, dress, articulate, and believe whatever I please. My usual fair attire consists primarily of brightly colored dresses or skirts, carefully accessorized with a scarf or various pieces of jewelry, and accompanied by bare feet or, on occasion, a pair of cowboy boots. I spend my days gamboling down dirt paths, ingesting lavish amounts of Greek and Indian food, engaging in pleasant conversation with strangers, and participating in free-verse poetry showcases. In my many years of winding through those beguiling trails, the Oregon Country Fair has woven itself into my natural disposition, creating a certain temperament that I carry with me wherever I go—an open mind, a big heart, eagerness to learn, and no inhibitions. That's how I live.

Jon Dean

None of us knew why we turned left at the road to Beaver Creek. Maybe it was because I yelled, "Left!" and Joe obliged my request with great enthusiasm. Maybe, though, it was calling to us, an irresistible magical spell that none of our fertile minds and weak willpower could possibly resist. We drove seven miles on snaking pavement. Then, abruptly, it changed from lush, green farmland to dense, dark forest that filled us with unimaginable excitement and glee as soon as our front tires hit the old, worn gravel road.

At this point, we weren't on Beaver Creek Road anymore; we were in the bowels of Beaver Creek, and could no longer escape its iron grip. The road continued on into the woods, twisting and turning as our hearts beat faster and faster with anticipation. After twenty minutes of continuous hairpin turns and deep potholes that scraped our undercarriage, the trees suddenly dispersed, and a magnificent clear-cut appeared before our eyes. Although depressing, this clear-cut filled us with a sort of wonder, and it became so silent it was as if Beaver Creek itself was withholding the sounds of the adventures beyond.

# My Friend, My Love, My Joseph

### Emiko Koike

I fell in love with Joseph. It's hard to believe that one can find love within forty-eight hours, but it happened to me. Excitement and adrenaline buzzed rapidly through my veins as black clouds shrouded the sky and waltzed with the roaring thunder. I'm not sure what took my breath away, the blustering wind or Joseph's beauty.

Joseph, a little town located in the northeast corner of Oregon, captured my attention with life-sized bronze statues, unique art, and vivacious citizens. The town gave me the opportunity to reconnect with nature. I watched the sunrise and sunset that seemed to burn mountaintops and frosty lakes with fire. During the day I ventured to local hotspot diners and shops, explored hiking trails, and enjoyed the sunny warmth. Daytime was not the only time to experience Joseph—in the evenings, my family and I drove the back roads during the constant thunderstorms, and this appeared to be a cue for the deer to dance with us. The four-legged beauties pranced through the high grass and the unusually warm rain.

I gasped as the thunder and lightning began their duet.

I was in love with Joseph.

# What Makes a Vacation in Oregon Special?

## Todd Davidson
### EXECUTIVE DIRECTOR OF TRAVEL OREGON

I am often asked which of Oregon's attributes and amenities makes it a more desirable travel destination. For all her beauty and diversity and vistas and experiences, what makes Oregon special...memorable... cherished?

On September 11, 2001, a plane full of female Japanese junior high school students were flying into Portland, Oregon, for a week-long educational study tour. The terrorist attacks of that tragic day resulted in their flight being rerouted to Vancouver, B.C.—but the efforts of the professionals at Azumano International, and an immediately dispatched motor coach, meant their trip across the Canadian border and on to Oregon was only delayed by a day. However, they were not allowed to bring their luggage.

This is when the magic began: their "homestay" families in Oregon met them at the school with clothing; retail stores stayed open late, offering the girls personal items and shoes; and the staff at attractions they visited in Oregon, knowing the girls were making up time for their lost day, presented them with popular souvenir items from their gift shops, as the time to shop was eliminated from the girls' tours.

One month after that tragic day, one thousand Oregonians traveled to New York to show America that travel was safe and that we were united as a country. I had the honor and privilege of traveling with this band of Oregonians, and experienced the gratitude of the New York hotel employees who were brought back from being furloughed because of the business we brought to their property. But nothing touched me more than the moment I met an elderly woman who was standing along the route of New

York's Columbus Day Parade. The Oregonians had been invited to walk in that parade—and the shouts from the crowd expressing their love and appreciation were overwhelming—but this one woman stood on the curb shaking the hand of every Oregonian she could reach. When she got to me, she held on. And then, as she embraced me, she whispered through her tears, "You have no idea what you all have done for me, for this city."

For all of Oregon's diverse natural beauty, amazing culinary offerings, abundant outdoor recreation, dynamic urban centers, cherished rural communities, and sweeping scenic vistas found along back roads throughout the state—to appreciative Japanese students, to the grateful tears of a New Yorker, and to millions of visitors who travel to Oregon each year on vacation from across the country and around the world—it is Oregonians themselves that are our greatest asset.

Fifty years from now, when Oregon celebrates her 200th birthday (and me my 100th) I hope we still value how special it is to be an Oregonian, and the tremendous opportunity we have to share our amazing corner of the world with our guests.

## Kelli Luke

A s a child, the thought of living in Oregon disappointed me. What was so special about Oregon? It wasn't like New York or California or Hawaii or one of those places that you always think of when people ask where you want to live when you grow up. California has its fame, New York has the whole city-life, Hawaii has its tropical feel, but what does Oregon have? Rain and Christmas trees? We even have a town called Boring. So, as I grew up, it never occurred to me that people could actually want to come to Oregon. That was, until I went to Gilchrist.

It happened so suddenly that, looking back now, I can't remember what a day would feel like without knowing that I have a half-brother. My mom and dad sat my brothers and me down in the living room and just let it come out without warning. "You have another brother," my mom said, quickly and to the point. Great, another brother, I thought, as she started to tell the story about my father and his ex-girlfriend, Ronda. As the only girl in the family, the last thing I wanted was another brother. Plus, Josh was older; nine years older. The last thing I wanted was an older brother to pick on me. But as much as I didn't want to admit it at first, I was excited to meet him. The next month, we decided to head out to Gilchrist, Oregon, to meet my half-brother for the first time.

The car ride from West Linn was long—four hours of questions and many unknown answers. Dad told us all about the small town that was forty minutes south of Bend, and apparently, if you blinked while driving through, you'd miss it completely. But even now, years after my first trip, I can still remember my first moments there vividly.

The nervousness grew as we saw a mailbox with the name Bishop on the side. My dad turned onto the long driveway, and there stood a small, one-story house. The lawn out front was as green as could be, with a trampoline right in the middle. Next to the house was a large garage with piles of wood stacked by it. As I stepped out of the truck, all I could smell was the air—the fresh, clean air. Thinking back to that moment, I would've never guessed that I would eventually love that place. But as the trip went on, I couldn't imagine how anyone wouldn't. And when it finally came to an end, I didn't want to leave.

In that one October weekend, I had fallen completely in love with Joshua and his family. Ever since, every trip I've taken there has given me amazing memories, like hunting for lost golf balls with Josh in the woods behind the house, and swimming in the stream in town after Josh's graduation. The little diner became my favorite place to eat, because it amazed me that everyone there knew one another. Gilchrist amazed me. The winters were always snowy, and the summers were always sweltering. Probably the best part of the whole experience was watching out the window as we drove from the rainy Willamette Valley to dry central Oregon. Everything around me changed, but it was still Oregon.

That was probably the one thing that changed my mind about my so-called-boring little state. From my experiences in that one small town, I learned to appreciate Oregon for what it really had: the mountains, the enormously tall trees, the fresh air, and the overall beauty of the great outdoors. Thanks to Gilchrist, I fell in love with Oregon.

## Susan Thompson

One day, when I was tired of hearing friends tell me how much it rains in Oregon, I reminded them that it only rains twice a year in Oregon: "The first time for six months, and the second time for six months!"

# Fell in Love with Oregon

*Jason Moore*

I was a musician living in Southern California. After seven years, the band I was in broke up and the lead guitarist left town. I found out he and his girlfriend moved to Southern Oregon. I took a week's vacation and caught a train to Klamath Falls, hoping to take a bus to Grants Pass (not knowing the size of Grants Pass) to try to find them. It turned out they were living on a gold-mining claim deep in the woods. They had just borrowed a friend's car to come down to check their mail, and got my letter the same day I arrived. They drove to Klamath Falls and found me at the bus station.

The minute I got to their claim, I fell in love with Oregon. I went back at the end of my week off, gave a month's notice, and moved back with them. I also mined for gold with them. We made enough money to buy new gear and form another band. I'm now a Portland resident, and have been working at Music Millennium for fourteen years. I love this state!

# The Oregon National Guard

*Lt. Col. Alisha Hamel*
OREGON NATIONAL GUARD

My name is Lt. Col. Alisha Hamel, and I joined the Oregon National Guard after I finished ROTC at Portland State University. Can you imagine going to PSU during the 1980s and having to wear your uniform on campus on Tuesdays? I solved that problem by not scheduling any classes except ROTC on Tuesdays.

Things are much different now. I deployed shortly after getting commissioned as a second lieutenant in the 206th Air Terminal Movement Control Detachment. We were the first Oregon Army Guardsmen to be deployed as a unit in forty-nine years. After I returned from my deployment to Saudi Arabia, my stepfather, a door gunner during Vietnam, thanked me and my fellow soldiers; for the first time, he was getting some respect for his own service because of our work. Our return to the United States was much more positive than his had been, because previous generations made sure we were treated better after our deployments were over.

The Oregon National Guard is now sending close to three thousand soldiers to Iraq. This is the largest deployment of soldiers from the Oregon National Guard since the 41st Infantry Division was activated in September 1940. These soldiers go because they volunteered to serve their country. I hope that Oregonians support them as well as they did when the 41st Infantry went during WWII, and when I went during Desert Storm.

The thing that I love most about being in the Oregon National Guard is that we are truly a cross-section of Oregonians. We are conservative, liberal, the good and the not-so-good. We are the best and brightest, and the ones who need a little extra help to make it through this life. We are all brothers and sisters. We are your brothers, sisters, aunts, uncles, mothers, fathers, neighbors. We are Oregonians, and we are so proud of that. Wherever we go, we brag about being from this wonderful state of Oregon. We are the best ambassadors for Oregon that we can be.

# Keeping It Fresh. Keeping It Oregon.

*Doug Zanger*

FOUNDER OF XHANG CREATIVE

One of the greatest things about Oregon is the food. There is no denying that it is the best on the planet. When I first moved here in 1992, I didn't really have as much appreciation for the bounty of Oregon as I do today. My family and I love going to the Beaverton Farmers' Market. We live very close to farm stores west of Murray Hill off of Scholls Ferry Road. As the seasons change, we have the opportunity to really feel (and taste) what Oregon has to offer. When the berries come out, we head out to Smith Berry Barn to pick. When the apples are harvested, we go to Oregon Heritage Farms to load up, and we do the same when it's time to pick our pumpkin for Halloween. When walnuts and hazelnuts call it a season, we visit Loughridge Farms. One of my favorite summer dishes is potato salad, using fresh reds from Baggenstos Farm. It makes me feel good to know that the potatoes are being grown just around the corner, and the taste is unmatched.

Though these observations are just about produce, every individual who works in agriculture works very hard to ensure that we have the very best. From fishing to ranching and everywhere in between, I can't think of a better group of people who are endlessly passionate about the possibilities of what we can raise and grow. Our agricultural industry is vibrant, and I'm sure that all of us want to keep it that way. We all can do our part by consistently supporting the industry. It's not just about buying Oregon; it's about sharing stories of everything that is so delicious about the state we all love so much.

# Mrs. Mabel's story, written by Rachel Kvamme

I had the pleasure of spending one Saturday morning in April 2009 getting to know Mrs. Mabel, a resident at Providence ElderPlace and an Oregon resident for almost all her life. In the few hours we spent together, I learned many things about Mrs. Mabel—including her love of reading (especially books about history and real people), her years working at a beauty salon in downtown Portland, her Scottish and Irish roots, and her preference as a child to play football with the boys rather than staying in the kitchen "cookin' biscuits" with her grandmother.

When Mrs. Mabel was born in 1926, Oregon had only been a state for sixty-seven years. Though she was born in North Dakota, Mrs. Mabel's family had moved to Boring, Oregon, by the time she started primary school. She lived with her mother, stepfather, and siblings (her biological father passed away when she was very young). At the age of fourteen, Mrs. Mabel and her family moved to Forest Grove, Oregon, where she attended Forest Grove Union High School and graduated in 1944. After graduation Mrs. Mabel moved to Portland and got a job as a hairdresser at the Master Wave Beauty Salon, which was then located downtown on SW 5th and Washington. The owner of the salon introduced her to his son and, on February 14, 1948 (Oregon's eighty-ninth anniversary), when Mrs. Mabel was twenty-one, they were married.

The next year, Mrs. Mabel had her first son. At age thirty-three, she had her second son. Though her sons were were eleven years apart, she says they were very close. Tragically, Mrs. Mabel's husband was killed in one war when he was just thirty-nine, and she later lost her eldest son to the Vietnam War.

After her husband's death, Mrs. Mabel worked very hard to raise her two sons as a single mother, telling herself, "'Get up out of this bed and take care of these boys because you have to do that. You can't sit there and feel sorry for yourself.' It was lucky that I had a profession because a lot of people don't have anything to turn to." She worked for fifteen years at her father-in-law's salon and then, after tiring of hairdressing, switched to working as a receptionist at a salon in Washington Square, where she worked until she retired at age sixty-five. In retirement, Mrs. Mabel worked as a volunteer for a few years in the cafeteria at Portland's Centennial Middle School, endearingly referred to as "The Taco Lady" by some of the students.

When asked what her favorite things about Oregon are, Mrs. Mabel replied, "I like the mountains and the rivers and the scenery here. I think it's a beautiful place to live. It's a beautiful state all over. It really is. We have everything—we have the rivers and the forests and the ocean. Ooh, the ocean is beautiful."

Although things just don't seem to her to be as safe as they used to be, and she usually regrets reading the newspaper because it's filled with sad stories, Mrs. Mabel told me that the one thing she loves to read about in the paper is news about the Portland Trail Blazers, whom she's been a fan of for "forever and a day." She vividly remembers when they won the championship in 1977: "That was a real big thing." Her favorite player used to be Clyde Drexler, but these days she likes Brandon Roy.

Ms. Mabel is one of 3,790,060 Oregon residents. From the bits and pieces of her life I was able to gather during our time together, it is clear to me that this woman is a shining example of the ordinary, but extraordinary, lives of those living in our state.

# Oregon the Beautiful

## Dena Hart

I was born and raised primarily in Bend, Oregon. Even as a child, I knew I was living in a special place. We lived on some land on the outskirts of town. I used to love walking to the airport when I was little. I would lay on my back and watch the planes. As I grew older, I never lost that interest. The crystal blue skies were so welcoming, they seemed to beckon the planes to visit.

Later, whether it was running up Pilot Butte for cross-country practice, or visiting any of the wonders of Oregon—Lava Butte, Crater Lake, Fort Rock (where we searched for many an arrowhead), skiing Mount Bachelor, or staying in our own yard, I felt very fortunate to be living in such a beautifully diverse state. I have moved away and lived back East and in the Southwest, and while those places have their own beauty, Oregon will always be my home.

# Finding Macksburg

*Dorothy Blackcrow Mack*

When I moved to Oregon in 1988, I went to the two-hundred-strong Mack Reunion. All the Macks, except my father, had stayed in Oregon; I grew up in Geneva, New York, drawn ever westward through my life to find my pioneer ancestors who founded Macksburg.

"Been to Macksburg yet?" one of my cousins asked me.

"No, I can't find it on the map."

"It's not on the map anymore, not since 1895 when it got swallowed up by Canby. We used to have Mack reunions there, down by the Mollala River, but we quit because nobody could find it."

I decided to find it, and settle where the W. O. Mack wagon train homesteaded after crossing the Plains on the Oregon Trail in 1852. On a Land Donation Claims map, I located the W. O. and F. P. Mack sections along the Mollala River between Canby and Mulino. W. O. Mack farmed 640 acres, founded Macksburg, and installed his son, my great-great-great-grandfather, Arthur Loring Mack, as the town's first postmaster.

I drove to Molino, passed the Molino Grange, and turned onto Macksburg Road. I imagined what my new address might be: Dorothy Mack, 101 Macksburg Road, Macksburg, Oregon. I meandered south until I found a "For Sale" sign in front of a small house with a mossy roof. I pulled into the overgrown yard and peered into the whitewashed dump.

I kept driving past trailers and manufactured homes set back in the trees along the river until I came to a crossroads, Macksburg and Elias. There were small houses on three corners, dwarfed by huge chestnut trees that were probably planted by W. O. On the fourth corner there was a wheat field where W. O.'s large farmhouse must have stood.

I followed Elias Road down to the river where W. O.'s land claim ended. I walked over polished river boulders and rutted sand, past rhododendron and willow bushes bent over by spring floods, new leaves pushing through nests of sticks caught among the branches. I imagined picnics under the alders and cottonwoods, and plank tables and benches set on sawhorses, laden with berry pies filled with berries from the riverbank. I imagined the lush rich land, a full harvest, and the feeling of respite after the hard work clearing stumps and stones from floodplain soil.

I continued south on Macksburg Road to the four acres W. O. had donated to the community for the Macksburg School, now empty, and the Macksburg Church and Cemetery, which are both still in use. Except for these, Macksburg no longer exists.

What caused Macksburg to disappear? W. O. must have worked his sons hard, because all eleven moved away—some continued farming near Scio and Stayton, while others hated farming and left it for teaching and clerking. W. O.'s land was sold long ago, and the old homestead moved to the Lutheran Church parking lot in Canby, now used as the Shalom Center for community meetings.

Much later I dined at the Sylvia Beach Hotel. The woman next to me saw my name tag. "Do you belong to the pioneer Mack family?"

"Yes," I said, "Arthur Loring branch."

"I grew up in Macksburg," she said, "and went to school there. My father and mother are buried there. I moved away, but I keep going back."

"Me, too," I said.

# A Place to Play

*Gail Balden*

In fifteen years of directing plays at the Coaster Theatre Playhouse on the Oregon coast, I've learned that what audiences really want to know is whether anything ever goes wrong backstage. Though fascinated with the world of make-believe, they're more interested in what it takes to create that world.

If anything can go wrong, it will. Windows won't open, so the burglar has to use the front door; the maid trips on her way offstage and falls down, smashing her tray of dishes; dogs lured across stage with biscuits stop and walk into the audience. Guns don't go off, the resulting pause finally causing someone backstage to scream "Bang!" Phones don't ring; the cast eats the food props, so pizza pieces have to be substituted for canapés. Actors walk off when they forget their lines, leaving the rest of the cast to clean up the missing pages of dialogue.

The Coaster Theatre Playhouse in downtown Cannon Beach, a rustic spot where none of the two hundred seats is a bad one, wasn't always a theatre. Built in the early 1920s and operated as a roller skating rink into the '50s, the barn-like building provided a place for folks to skate to the music of a calliope. They skated all day and evening for thirty-five cents. One day a week, the skating rink was used as a silent movie theater.

In the mid-1960s, a local realtor, Richard Atherton, who dreamed of bringing professional theater to town, purchased the building. The junk stored inside was burned, and kids were sent into the rafters to kick down pigeon poop. Local work crews removed Flash Gordon movie posters found beneath the wallpaper. Old Cannon Beach streetlights served as lighting. The first performance after the transformation was violinist Paul Bellum, director of the Portland Chamber Orchestra. Atherton, Stan Glarum, musical director for Lewis and Clark College, and Fred Kline, head of the Art Department at Portland State, brought the Haystack Program to Cannon

Beach. Portland State's Summer Stock Company, a feature of the program, began performances in 1969. When the United States landed a man on the moon that summer, one performance was delayed so everyone could watch the landing on television.

Maurie Clark, a Portland patron of the arts, purchased the building in 1972 and changed the location of the stage to the east side of the theater, and the floor to a sloping one with tiered seating. He added a proscenium arch to the front of the stage. The renovation crew couldn't sand out the figure-eight skating designs laid down on the maple floor in the early '30s, so they left them in as a visible piece of history.

The Coaster Theatre Playhouse, one of the longest-standing landmarks on the Oregon coast, is now in its thirty-seventh year and continues to provide year-round entertainment. The echoes of skaters swooshing around the rink, the words and music of hundreds of performing artists who brought audiences to tears and laughter, and the applause of thousands who passed through its doors, still linger in the air.

# Oregon Born and Bred

*Teresa Carroll*

I was born at Emanuel Hospital in November of 1956 and have lived in the Portland area my entire life. The same doctor who delivered me and my three brothers in 1955, 1956, 1959, and 1962, also delivered my son in January 1977. I have traveled to other places while serving in the U.S. Army, but nothing I have seen compares to home, and I know that the Portland area will be my final resting place when the time comes. It's already the final resting place of my parents, both sets of my grandparents, and numerous aunts, uncles, and other family members.

Our family tent-camped a lot while I was growing up both at the beach (Cape Lookout State Park and Fort Stephens were favorites) and in the mountains at various campgrounds in the Mount Hood National Forest. I remember many summer visits to the Tillamook Cheese Factory, the Pioneer Museum, and the wreck of the *Peter Iredale*, just to name a few. I can't think of any place I would rather be than here, where I can travel an hour in either direction and enjoy two totally different places.

I love the rain and wouldn't trade the Oregon weather for anything. The weather is great most of the time, except when we hit the extremes in heat or cold. When people who transplanted here complain about the weather, I suggest that if they don't like it, they should return where they came from. It's perfect here. I was here for the Columbus Day storm, Mount St. Helens' eruption, and the floods of 1996.

I am proud to say that I am a native Oregonian, and my jeep's custom plates confirm it: "OR N8IV."

# Patrick Broderick

The year was 1957, and the month was October—two days before deer season was to begin. Two "down-and-outers," Donald Lee Ferguson and Jessie Thurman Hibdon, found themselves in Paisley, Oregon, with a great need for money. The postmistress, Anita Bannister, noticed the two men as they walked in the door of the building that served as both the general store and the post office. They were dressed like cowboys, and appeared to be drunk.

They carried guns up to her and demanded "the payroll." The two desperados did not know that the mill had recently closed and there was no payroll. They demanded and got what was available to Mrs. Bannister, which consisted of mostly change and money orders. Mr. Hibdon left the scene of the crime first, while Ferguson remained inside to warn the locals not to pursue.

One of the witnesses of the hold-up slipped out while the robbery was in progress. When he got outside he yelled for help. A plumber, sixty-five-year-old Troy Lawson, was outside near his truck when he heard the cry. It was close to hunting season, and Mr. Lawson had a hunting rifle in the back window of his pickup. While moving toward the crime scene, Lawson was noticed by Hibdon. Hibdon shot him in the abdomen with the first shot, and the second shot blew a hole in the front wall of the post office. Lawson was mortally wounded.

The two robbers escaped in their car and were pursued by a posse, which caught up to them at a hastily formed barricade near Summer Lake Lodge. As the two bandits jumped out of their vehicle, Ferguson was shot by the posse. Although he survived, his days of evil deeds were up.

However, Hibdon escaped into the tree line, and the pursuit was on. He discarded his rifle and continued northeast for nearly seventy-five miles, avoiding roads until he came to the Jack Pine Motel, about ten miles south of LaPine. There he purchased a straight razor and a few candy bars with coins and then disappeared into the woods across the road.

The robbery and murder took place on a Thursday. The next Tuesday, my father, Harold Broderick, my brother, Bud, and I stopped by the Jack Pine Motel for fuel and supplies. We were hunting about five miles to the north and were "regulars" in the area. The owner of the motel told us of the unusual visitor the afternoon before, and after some discussion the state police were alerted.

The next day we went on a midday hunt with the sole purpose of letting me be on a "stand" for the first time with my rifle. I was twelve years old. My dad and brother placed me against a fence post at the end of a meadow with instructions to load no shell into the barrel unless about to shoot, and never to do so while walking. My dad and brother moved around the tree line in opposite directions with the hope of driving a buck into the meadow and allowing a shot for me.

A couple of hours went by, and I was eager to get out of there and go back to camp for dinner, but I had instructions not to move. So I did not move.

I was startled when I heard my dad yell, "Halt or I will shoot!" I turned around to see a man standing a couple of feet behind me and the fence post. I then saw my dad had "leveled" his rifle at the man and he once again yelled, "One more step, and you are dead."

The man stopped. My dad moved toward me and told me to take my rifle back to the truck and empty it of all rounds. He also told me to honk the truck horn with three long blasts. Three horn blasts, or three blasts from a gun, was an emergency signal that would bring anyone within hearing to the source of the sound. Shortly after the three blasts, I heard my very large brother crashing through the trees to the truck. When he got there he was frightened and more than a little upset at me for blowing the horn.

I explained what I had witnessed a couple hundred feet away in the end of the meadow. We moved cautiously to my dad's location, only to find the man "spread-eagled" against the fence post. My dad was ten feet away, with his 30.06 pointed at the man's back. We then moved slowly to the truck, where my brother tied the man's hands together behind his back and his feet together as well. My dad climbed in the front of the truck cap, next to the truck's cab. The man's hands were then tied to the tailgate chains, and Dad instructed us to drive slowly back to our camp, on our way to highway 26 and a pay phone. The man had not said a word to this point, and as I peered through the back window of the truck my brother kept saying, "The old man has lost it."

When we stopped by the camp, we were next to a small stream. At this point the man broke his silence and asked for a drink of water. I was instructed to get a saucepan, dip it in the stream, and offer it to our mysterious rider. I was nervous, but I somehow held the saucepan as he drank one pan of water and then another. Then we continued another two miles to the Jack Pine Motel and a pay phone. When we got there, the proprietor recognized this man as the guy who had stopped by the previous afternoon.

The Oregon State Police were called, and two patrol cars arrived an hour later from Bend. We watched as the two policemen searched the man and found two pockets of change and the missing money orders. They identified him as Jessie Thurmond Hibdon.

About that time, a "stringer" for *The Oregonian* and the *Oregon Journal* showed up and asked for some pictures. Several pictures were taken of Hibdon secured in the patrol car. The stringer asked me if I would sit on the ground next to Hibdon and have my picture taken with him. I reluctantly did so. The next morning, on the front pages of both papers, there was a photo of Hibdon and me with the headline: HAMMOND VOLUNTEER FIRE CHIEF CATCHES MURDERER. The caption under the picture was very embarrassing. It read, "This is one scared 12-year-old."

As I look back on it now, some fifty years later, I realize that, if my dad had not seen that man sneaking up on me, I would have willingly given him my rifle if he had asked.

My dad received several over-the-phone interviews from crime magazines. He told them all the same thing, but everyone wrote a different story. He was told that he would have received a $10,000 reward from the USPS if Hibdon had remained on the loose for another twenty-four hours.

That was my family's fifteen minutes of fame. I still have the rope that tied Hibdon to the tailgate.

# On the Farm in the Mid-Twentieth Century

*Robert Mumby*

During World War II, my father sold his Farmer's Market drug store in Los Angeles and brought my mother, my brother, and me to Roseburg. Shortly thereafter, we moved to a ranch some sixteen miles of paved, gravel, and dirt road west of Roseburg at the base of the Coast Range.

Two brothers, immigrants from Sweden, sold the farm to my father. On about one thousand acres of land they raised cattle, sheep, pigs, chickens, and turkeys; grew prunes, plums, wheat, and hay; and harvested and milled the second-growth Douglas fir forest on the hillsides. There was also an apple orchard and a giant black walnut tree, and vegetable gardens were planted behind the houses.

Each brother had a house with an outhouse—there was no indoor plumbing. My mom's first priority was to change that, especially after I fell off the footbridge into the creek while running back home from the out-house. Communications were a bit behind the times, too. For the first few years our phone was in a wooden cabinet hanging on the wall. You turned a crank to make a call. Six homes shared one "party" line.

All those different animals and crops were too much for us to tend. I was two years old and my brother was nine, so we couldn't help much. The turkeys were the first to go—so dumb they required constant watching and care to survive. The little saw mill was closed and a "gypo" logging outfit was contracted to cut and haul out the firs. The chicken flock got smaller, and the sheep were eventually sold.

It was hard going after the war, when prices and agricultural demand fell. Friends from Los Angeles kept coming by to stay a few days and experience the country life. Meat was to be sold, not eaten by family and friends, so my dad packed a .22 revolver while doing the farm work; city visitors were often treated to venison. If they came during the salmon run, they got fish. (At that time salmon came up the larger creek to spawn. No more.)

I had a great time with my two dogs, exploring and exploiting the farm. We hunted ground squirrels, looked for salamanders in the two creeks running through our property, tried to ride the calves, and captured raccoons and owls, although we failed to tame them as additional pets. Blackie, the sheepdog, helped me round up the cows for milking, and Pluto, the mutt, tried to dig squirrels out of their burrows. Much of the time he had bite marks on his nose.

School for first through eighth grades was a three-classroom building across the bridge from the Umpqua Store and prune dryer. The other kids picked on me because I was from California, which was almost as bad as being an "Okie" from the Dust Belt. Luckily I had a big brother to intervene. The experience of being an unwelcome outsider may have been what helped me become more tolerant of people, no matter where they are from, what color they are, or religion they have.

We stayed on the farm for about ten years. During that time I learned that farmers made a good community. Despite dislikes and occasional conflicts, they helped each other out, working together to raise crops, livestock, and families.

# It's Raining, It's Raining!

*Lt. Col. Alisha Hamel*

It was August 1990, and I had just found a job after getting my degree from Portland State University and going to my officer basic course for the Oregon National Guard. I had this job for just one week when I was called up to go to Desert Storm. The 206th Air Terminal Movement Control Detachment was the first National Guard unit to be called up in Oregon in 49 years.

We arrived in Riyadh, Saudi Arabia, on September 15th—and it was hot! We walked off the plane and just sat down on the edge of the runway waiting for orders as to what to do next. Amazingly enough, they didn't even know we were coming, so they didn't know what to do with us. We waited and waited. We spent one night in the underground garage of the Saudi defense building with the lights on for the whole twenty-four hours and the typical hole in the floor for a bathroom. It was stinky and very bright. We were very happy to get out of there and head to Dhahran.

We had one soldier go down with heat stroke on the way to Dhahran, and we were all still very hot. We arrived in Dhahran and spent a week or so at Camp Jack in the very fine sand of the Saudi desert that puffed up whenever anyone walked in it. We then moved to a warehouse without walls on the Damman port where there was at least a chance of a breeze, and it was all paved, so there was no sand.

There was one more move to a military camp next to Damman port where we had actual rooms (four people to a room that should only hold one person). All this time there was no rain, no hint of rain, not even a little spit of rain. There was barely even a cloud in the sky. You can imagine that this was very hard on a little unit from the western part of Oregon. We love the sun, but there has to be a little rain to appreciate it even better. We actually started to get depressed that there was so much sun. Where was the rain? Would it never rain?

Finally in January, there was a little cloud on the horizon. The beginning of the offensive against Iraq was also almost ready to start. The little cloud became bigger. The Oregon National Guardsmen started to notice the air was getting cooler and...wetter? Could we possibly have a little rain? The cloud got bigger, then bigger. The Oregonians started to get more animated. They started to go to the windows to see if we were going to get rain.

The first droplets started to fall. An excited murmur ran through the Oregonians. First one, then another, started to go outside. The rain started to come down a little faster, then faster. The Oregonians started to run outside. "It's raining, it's raining," exclaimed the Oregon National Guardsmen, jumping for joy. They started to dance and sing. An Oregon rain dance happened right there. The Oregonians were so happy that they could even appreciate the sun again. Western Oregonians need rain. It reminded us of home. The wet Oregonians slowly, slowly made their way back inside. The war had begun against Iraq.

# Grape Lane Poultry Farm, an Original Oregon Pioneer Farm

*Jayne Miller*

G rape Lane Poultry Farm is an original Oregon pioneer farm. It was settled first by the Calapulia and next by William Frazer after he arrived on the first wagon train to Oregon in 1843. In 1901 the first permitted building was constructed: a rare and still standing two-story brooder chicken house. In 1915, my husband's family traded land grants for the farm. In 1926, Mrs. Davis—who had been born in the house—stated that the portion of the house she was standing in was almost one hundred years old.

In 2000, my husband and I inherited the now-worn remnants of the farm, which appeared to be as worn as I was from a life of corporate America. The last ten acres included the original farm home, the two-story brooder house, and other 1800s buildings, as well as the Calapulia site. Entering the home, untouched for almost one hundred years, was as if I had walked back in time. There were collections of antique farm photos, tools, feed-sack clothing, and feed sacks from as early as the 1800s on up to the 1970s. Newspapers from the 1800s up to the lunar landing, farm receipts from the 1800s, and much more. The family never threw a thing out. The untouched history of this once large and productive farm inspired me to catch my breath and redirect my life as that of a small sustainable farmer. I had grown up on my parent's 7,000-acre cattle ranch, so I was not too unfamiliar with a life on a farm.

We decided to save the farm and re-homestead it as an Oregon Tilth Organic farm. And in spite of the declining water table and Measure 37 encroachment, we hung on. Unable to find good employment and weary and ill from the corporate hassle, I found my better self in the farm. Of the seven grants I wrote, I was awarded five to help revitalize the farm. By my own hands, I planted nearly one thousand native riparian trees and shrubs to enhance our pristine upland savanna woodland and increase wildlife. I received an award for that work, and the blisters have been well worth it. I grow grain and harvest it by hand, sprouting some for making our own bread, crackers, pancakes, and muffins, saving the rest for planting. I harvest pears from our one-hundred-year-old pear trees and make pear butter; I collect the nuts from twenty-one walnut trees and make fantastic walnut butter. The three antique apple trees yield outstanding fall and winter apples. I dry the plums from the plum trees and freeze the berries.

But the garlic takes center stage. In the year 2000, there were only six plants left of a rare, hot, and, in some cases, larger-than-elephant-garlic plant carried here by an unknown pioneer in the 1800s. I taught my horse to plow the herb and garlic fields, which are pollinated by the bees I raise, and I hold workshops that give people hope by teaching them to live sustainable lives.

# Pickin'

*Sandra Ellston*

The taste of toothpaste at 5 AM is enough to induce vomiting. My lunch was made last night: a hefty sandwich, a frozen Snickers bar, and pop, frozen too, so it will still be icy at noon. There is gossip to talk about with the girls on the bus as we prop our cutoff-clad knees against the seat in front of us, and there are flirtations to pursue with the migrant boys. I know just enough Spanish to catch when they're talking about us. Even with flirting, they pick twice as many berries as we do. They crouch by the rows and their hands move swiftly, flicking the berries into carriers. We girls begin by straddling the rows and twisting each berry from the stem; we progress to eating more than we put in our hallecks and end by sitting in the dirt rows, moving along by shuffling our buttocks in a sluggish walk. When the sun is high, off comes Dad's old shirt, and we work on our tans, dangerously blistering our shoulders. After lunch, we goof off and make enormous strawberry wounds on each other in battle. We return filthy and giddy from a day too good to have missed.

# Grandpa's Jackknife

*Gentry Cutsforth*

Early Oregon farm stories tell us of all the wonderful things Grandma did with her long apron. Useful things, like gathering eggs, vegetables, and kindling chips; dusting and polishing the furniture; using it as a pot holder; wiping the baby's nose; and shooing the pigs out of the garden.

But what about Grandpa? Did he have a "jack-of-all trades" tool? Yes, indeed! Grandpa had his jackknife.

I remember Grandpa sitting in his favorite chair, his jackknife in hand, whittling toys and whistles for the grandkids, or using his trusty knife to fix Grandma's electric iron, toaster, or other gadgets—stopping now and then to whittle off a chaw from his plug of "tobaccy."

Around the barn, Grandpa's jackknife cut the strings on the bales of hay and straw, cut the leather hides into strips to fix the harness and saddles, or cut out leather half-soles to repair the family's shoes. Grandpa always carried the short stub of a flat carpenter's pencil in his shirt pocket and kept it meticulously sharpened with his knife. Knives were never invented to be used as toothpicks, but he didn't know that. And if Grandma hadn't shortened those new bib overalls, he would get out his knife and cut off the legs before stuffing them in his rubber boots.

At lambing or piggy time, the jackknife was sharpened and held over a match to sterilize it before using it as a veterinarian's instrument to castrate the young males. It was his skinning and butchering tool at slaughter time. It cut the pork fat into cubes for rendering into lard. He used it to trim and fillet summer caught salmon that would hang in the smoke house for days. That old knife opened filberts and walnuts, peeled and sliced crisp fall apples, sliced smoked ham and bacon, and shaved deer jerky into tasty slivers for everyone to sample.

He used a kraut cutter to shred cabbage for sauerkraut, but his jackknife was used first to cut and trim the excess leaves right in the garden, and slice the cabbage cores into thin slabs that were cool and tasty.

On a weekly basis, he cleaned and trimmed his fingernails, toenails, and corns with great care and dexterity. Of course, he never cleaned the knife after each use, but we tried not to think about that!

I don't know what Grandpa would have done without his jackknife on those yearly deer-hunting trips to eastern Oregon. It cut the kindling for the early morning bonfire that kept the big camp pot of black coffee steaming hot. It cut the long willow sticks, sharpened to a razor point, for roasting marshmallows, hot dogs, and toasted bread.

No matter where he went, Grandpa always carried a small box of wooden (farmer) matches, his carpenter pencil, a small whetstone, and his all-time, all-purpose instrument—his jackknife. The only other tool that had so many uses was the wooden-handled claw hammer that hung at his side. But that's another story!

# A Glimpse of Elk City

## Alexis Steenkolk

I live on the outskirts of Toledo where the pavement meets a one-way gravel road. Elk City is a small jewel that lies fifteen miles off the Newport ocean shore. I was raised out towards the countryside in a sturdy house built on love. My name is carved in the bridge below my house, along with those of the many Steenkolks before my generation. My family is made of hardworking men with Skoal cans imprinted in the back pocket of their jeans. Every morning, my relatives meet for coffee at the family gas station, just to BS.

Fresh-cut grass fills the clean summer air as I take the time and cherish my surroundings. With our property extending for acres, my possibilities are infinite. I have spent every summer riding quads through open cow pastures and fishing on our dock. The aroma of my grandma's fresh home-made apple pies reminds me of popsicle-stained faces and running through the sprinkler. Walking down the road to get the mail, my Bopa taught me how to shoot my first .22 by aiming at tin cans in the river. On rainy nights, my cousins and I would throw on our boots to go frog hunting and play in huge puddles. Year after year, I spent many unforgettable summers swimming in the river and making tree forts. My scars are just small reminders of all my favorite childhood memories. The countryside is where my heart belongs.

# Sweet Memories Growing Up on the Oregon Slope

*Kevin Trees*

I lay in bed looking out the window, listening to the meadowlarks singing in the cool, crisp, clean air not too far from my open bedroom window, and to the sound of the double-decker crop dusters spraying the onion and potato fields surrounding the house. I listened to all the other sounds in the distance as well—the cows, the dogs, the roosters, and the sweet music of the low putt-putt-putt of the two-cylinder tractors. I could also hear Dad running the saw in the shop, making more cabinets for another house or two that he was building. The aroma of eggs, hash browns, and toast or pancakes that Mother was making for breakfast could be smelled throughout the house. Mom would then call everyone to breakfast. My brothers and I came into the kitchen from all directions, from downstairs, the living room, outside, and the bedrooms.

After breakfast, we would all go our separate ways. I would be on my way down the hill on my green bike with a banana seat and sissy bar, wearing old jean cutoffs and shoes with no socks. My fawn-colored Great Dane following right behind, I would meet up with my buddy Billy to finish our fort and trails in the thick cattails along the road. When we got tired of catching snakes and frogs and fighting off the red-winged blackbirds that were nesting in the cattails, we would ride our bikes down the road another half-mile or so to the next neighbor's house and play with the kids in an old buckboard wagon under the big oak tree. In order for us to get to the wagon, one of us would have to distract the bulls while the rest of us would run out to the wagon. We would pretend that the bulls were Indians and they had just ambushed our wagon train. Some of us would be under the wagon, and the others would be in the bed of the wagon, shooting the bulls and cows with our BB guns. The more we shot the bulls, the more aggressive they became with their attack on our wagon train.

Some days, my brothers and I would ride our bikes just a short mile and a half to Grandma's. She would always meet us at the door with a sparkle in her eyes and a droopy smile on her soft, wrinkled face caused by the Bell's Palsy that she had from when she was young. Grandma's house always smelled the same—you could smell the yeast and fresh-baked bread and dinner rolls, or the smell of pies, and she would usually have fresh warm orange knots for us. On the days I mowed her lawn I always got twice as many, along with a big tall glass of cold milk. Sometimes in the summer I would go with Grandpa to the bull range, and we would go to the auction yard across the road and buy bulls or get in one of his semitrucks and take a two- or three-day trip to pick up bulls that he had purchased earlier in the week.

On other days, we would ride our bikes all day long on the ditch banks, stopping at friends' houses, or going up to the cousins' place to play at the pond. As the summer would heat up in the afternoon or evening, we would get some big dust storms or thunderstorms with fifty- to sixty-mile-an-hour winds, and then we would spend the next hour after the storm gathering up our aluminum lawn chairs and toys that were scattered all over the countryside. On the hot afternoons, after helping my friends buck hay so they could play sooner, we would spend hours playing and swimming in the ditch to cool off after throwing and stacking the hay. Some days I would help the neighbor run his dairy cows through the milk barn.

The winters were just as much fun. Back then we would get a lot of snow every year. I remember sitting at the kitchen table on Thanksgiving break and looking out the window, watching the farmers across the fields trying to harvest the sugar beets with the snow coming down hard and the wind blowing. That was the nice thing about living on the top of a big hill—you could see for miles and miles in all directions, and the scenery year-round—spring with the fields in different stages, some green and some just planted, and some fields just turned. In the winter, rolling hills covered in snow, everything white—I always pictured that this is what heaven looked like, all pure, and the horses and cattle roaming around in the white fields. But I'd soon realize that we were far from heaven; within hours the white fields would turn brown and mucky where the animals had trampled. This was back in the day when we got lots of snow every year, and the Snake River would flood somewhere along the banks between Adrian and Farewell Bend State Park, and as soon as there was enough snow, Dad would pull out the old blue-and-white Polaris snowmobile, and we would run all day long across the fields, along the ditch banks, and down the roads, until bare spots started showing through the snow.

Don't get me wrong; it was not all fun and games being the sons of a carpenter—we worked plenty. Sometimes on days that might reach 110 degrees, we might be pouring footings or foundations and have to hold the hot rebar up in place as we poured concrete, or we might be roofing the house with the hot sun pounding down on the tar paper and shingles, and in the late afternoon or evening I would go home and run through the sprinklers to cool off. Then, in the winter, we might be doing the same work, but with the temperatures below freezing, and sometimes with the wind chill you were looking at temperatures way below zero, and it would take hours to warm up after getting home. The one of us who got to the house first would be the one who got to warm up first in the bath; the rest would have to stand by the fireplace. I always liked to get the first warm bath and then go downstairs to sit by the fireplace.

I often long to go back in time and live it as a kid again. That was the life. This country would be a much better place if we still lived and shared the same values today that we lived and shared back in the day.

# Oregon in 2059: Forecasting the Past

## A look at the state of Oregon fifty years from now

## Ethan Seltzer

Professor, Toulan School of Urban Studies and Planning,
Portland State University

The great thing about history is that it has already happened. We may not agree about what it means, how things happened, why they happened, or even what the outcomes were, but time once passed does not pass again. At least we know that is true.

Forecasting the future is a bit trickier. No one knows what the future will bring. Sure, we might have some pretty well-informed guesses about what may happen, but odds are those guesses won't be very accurate. Today, in 2059, we want the future to be better than the last fifty years, but how can we ever top the Four Campaigns?

In 2009, Oregonians faced what seemed like overwhelming problems, as did people living in most places in the United States. We were part of a global knowledge economy that required creativity and innovation, but we weren't sure how to prepare all of our citizens for it, or how to include them all in it. The conflicting interests of urban and rural residents created an ideological divide that seemed unbridgeable.

Climate change not only threatened to alter ecosystems but also had nearby Western states clamoring for their share of Oregon's water and renewable energy resources. In early 2009, the magnitude of the fiscal mess that began with the financial crisis of 2008 became clear when early revenue projections for the 2009 Oregon legislative session showed massive shortfalls in state revenue in the coming biennium.

At the state level, the prospects for maintaining basic services and commitments looked bleak, so bleak that twentieth-century solutions to economic downturns—blasting open urban growth boundaries, creating new giveaways for any out-of-state corporation promising a few jobs,

241

funding a plethora of new highway interchange projects—promised little in the way of relief.

For a time, we tried to address these problems one task force at a time. Soon, however, it became apparent that the "war on..." approach was destined to fail. In fact, using baldly truculent terms as metaphors for the action needed obscured the real aim: the creation of solutions. Someone—nobody remembers who—suggested the term "campaign." This notion resonated with Oregonians for several reasons.

A campaign pursues something proactively. It is not a reaction, but a step toward a goal. It is purposeful, intentional, and forward-looking, the basis for all of the innovations that Oregon had become known for by 2009—the bottle bill, light-rail transit, bikes, urban growth boundaries, alternative energy, and more. In addition, winning campaigns are participatory—they can't succeed without a broad base of engagement. In short, campaigns are bridges to our aspirations, connecting us from where we are to where we want to be.

In 2012, we took a deep breath, and the Four Campaigns were born. The first was the Campaign for a Living Landscape. People began to realize that Oregon's sense of place was constructed not out of what we'd built or what we'd found, but out of the interplay among the working, wild, and urban landscapes throughout the state. Cities in nature and nature in the cities had become a vital calling card that attracted visitors and talented new residents to Oregon's metropolitan areas. Our food, wine, and forest products were sought after worldwide; "Made in Oregon" was a desirable brand, synonymous with quality, sustainability, and healthy living.

Through this campaign, Oregonians worked hard to modernize farm and forest enterprises, leveraging resources by developing new ways to make products that the world wanted while preserving the quality of the soil, water, and habitat that had given the state its sense of promise and opportunity. The term "Oregon-grown" became synonymous with food and fiber products that met the highest standards of sustainability and healthfulness. Oregon exported not just products and commodities, but production methods that weren't being used anywhere else in the world.

In an unexpected twist, growing food and fiber in these innovative ways created healthy ecosystems that began to provide tangible benefits to our cities and rural communities. The air and water were cleaner, and the landscape was better able to cope with the changes brought about by urban development. These "ecosystem services," previously unaccounted for and undervalued, became the core of a new set of urban/rural relationships that improved the economic and environmental health of communities in both regions. The perception that environment competed with economy was dispelled, as it became apparent that maintaining the productivity of farms and forests, preserving the health of natural habitats, and improving the efficiency of cities were all interrelated.

This first campaign quickly led to the second, the Campaign for Local Solutions, an economic incentive program that spawned a statewide network of innovative start-ups offering products and services to meet the everyday needs of Oregonians. New Oregon enterprises, developed with an eye toward long-term viability and responsiveness to local needs, ushered in a new and more stable period for Oregon communities, in what continued to be turbulent economic times just about everywhere outside our borders.

Scores of jobs were created, and wealth stayed local, as Oregonians bought electric cars built in Salem. These cars were powered by electricity generated at biomass plants using "Made in Oregon" generators that burned refuse from Oregon cities—a closed-loop process developed and patented by Oregonians. With the state as a true living laboratory for the world, Oregon's green economy took an exponential and very profitable leap onto the world stage. Through local excellence, Oregon achieved greater and more profitable global reach, and the state became truly self-sufficient in the process.

To support the first two campaigns, the Campaign for Creativity was launched. This campaign recognized that good ideas for creating desirable and sustainable places, managing working and wild landscapes, and doing more with less in fields ranging from sports apparel to lumber and wood products would be key to Oregon's global competitiveness. It was all about ideas, both for capturing markets and for making great spaces.

It was young bicyclists who figured out how to make bicycle commuting safe and attractive, and receptive city governments gave their ideas room to take hold. Working together, these groups created a model of "green and safe" bike lanes, convenient bike parking, and financial incentives for bike commuting that drew the attention of cities around the world.

Similarly, it was cutting-edge designers at Nike who, after many years, created a completely recyclable shoe. Over beers at a brewpub and later at a conference at Oregon State University, their manufacturing process got the attention of researchers in the Forestry School, and the Oregon zero-waste construction system—building houses in a manner that incorporates what used to be considered waste or scrap in the final structure—captured almost the entire new-home construction market.

Of course, connecting the dots among all of these campaigns was the fourth great effort, the Campaign for the Future. This campaign was about people, and it focused almost entirely on learning and education reform. True reform took place when the citizens of Oregon, recognizing that a high school education was hardly sufficient even if it was world-class, enacted a sales tax dedicated to public education that finally ended the roller coaster of funding and reforms that had plagued the state for decades.

The state's grade schools, high schools, and universities became the envy of the nation, as Oregon once again became recognized for having the best-prepared workforce in the world. Unlike in the twentieth century, when educational attainment in Oregon was largely a function of people—educated elsewhere—who were migrating to the state, educational attainment in 2059 can be directly traced to the engagement of Oregon residents with the much-admired Oregon Educational System, another coveted Beaver State brand.

Oregon thrives in 2059 not because it has become a spaceport, or because it has discovered a mushroom that halts aging, or because buildings no longer need steel and concrete to reach heights of half a mile. Instead, Oregon thrives because it has combined the Four Campaigns into an integral whole. By engaging each other beneath the banner of the campaigns, Oregonians found the way and the will to transcend the seemingly insurmountable challenges of 2009 in unique and authentically Oregonian ways.

In 2059, Oregon has become internationally known for directly benefiting from small groups of people getting together to change industries, communities, and institutions. What began as a "do it yourself "ethic pioneered by artists and musicians in the 1990s has blossomed to define an Oregon approach to problem solving and innovation. Its roots are in strong communities, and strong communities have empowered their residents to join together in new collaborations, able to tackle landscape-scale challenges without fear of losing identity or control.

Oregon thrives in 2059 because it has developed a new compact that empowers every one of its residents to make a good life without sacrificing the sustainability of the place or the interests of other people in the process. In 2059, the basic and historic notion about Oregon as a place for living a good life remains true. Today, by achieving local excellence, Oregon has actually achieved global reach. Oregon thrives, in short, because it has reasserted an old idea—"we're all in this together"—in new and innovative ways.

# Ooligan Press

Ooligan Press takes its name from a Native American word for the common smelt or candlefish. Ooligan is a general trade press rooted in the rich literary life of Portland and the Department of English at Portland State University. Ooligan is staffed by students pursuing masters degrees in an apprenticeship program under the guidance of a core faculty of publishing professionals.

**PROJECT MANAGERS:**
Leah Paul
Shannon Baraff
Rachel Moore

**DESIGN MANAGERS:**
Cory Freeman
Ellery Harvey

**COVER DESIGN:**
Elisabeth Wilson

**INTERIOR DESIGN:**
Andrew Wicker
Chory Ferguson

**MARKETING MANAGERS:**
Alex Tucker
Cara O'Neil

**MARKETERS:**
Brian Smith
Candice Peaslee
Cheri Woods-Edwin
Kerri Higby
Rachel Moore

**LEAD PROJECT EDITOR:**
Julie Franks

**LEAD EDITORS:**
Dehlia McCobb
Katie Shaw

**EDITING TEAM:**
Caroline Knecht
Chelle Dey
Chelsea Harlan
Dan Chabon
Devon Riley
Jessicah Carver
Jim Welsh
Kathryn Foster
Katie Lucas
Katy Drawhorn
Kay Tracy
Kenny Hanour
Lauren Saxton
Leah Brown
Lucy Softich
Marianna Hane Wiles
Mary E. Darcy
Maureen S. Inouye
Mike Munkvold
Sandra Arguello

# Colophon

O*regon Stories* was designed in Adobe InDesign CS4, alternating between Apple iMac G5s and a PC powered by an Intel Core 2 Duo 3.0 Ghz processor. The part title graphics were designed in Adobe Illustrator CS4 to coordinate with Wieden+Kennedy's Oregon 150 Commission logo.

The body text and author names are set in Adobe Jenson Pro with the occasional employment of its wonderfully stylized ligatures and italic swash capitals. In 1996, Adobe Systems released Adobe Jenson Pro, designed by Richard Slimbach based on a Venetian old style text face created by Nicolas Jenson in 1470. The body text is set in 11-point type on 13.5 points of leading. The author names are set in 16-point italic.

The story titles, section titles (in the text and in the table of contents), and the folios are set in Avenir LT Standard, employed to create cohesion with the cover design of Elisabeth Wilson. Avenir is a geometric sans-serif typeface designed by Adrian Frutiger in 1988. The word *avenir* is French for "future," and the typeface takes for its inspiration both the Erbar and Futura typefaces.

The blending of a typeface originally designed in the fifteenth century with one that carries the future in its very name allows *Oregon Stories*, by design, to punctuate the decades from Oregon's storied past into its as-yet-unwritten future.

The accent gray is black set at 55% density to match the tones of shadowless December days on the Oregon coast, and the silvery scaled skin of the spring Chinook.

The spatial relation of the text frame to the page is relative to the state of Oregon's width and height—as measured at its widest points—giving the page generous amounts of white space, bringing to mind the rolling, open hills of the Willamette Valley and sweeping wheat-fields of Oregon's eastern plateau.